Shul Going

Shul Going

*2500 Years of Impressions and
Reflections on Visits to the Synagogue*

CHARLES HELLER

RESOURCE *Publications* · Eugene, Oregon

SHUL GOING
2500 Years of Impressions and Reflections on Visits to the Synagogue

Resource Publications
An Imprint of Wipf and Stock Publishers
199 W. 8th Ave., Suite 3
Eugene, OR 97401

www.wipfandstock.com

PAPERBACK ISBN: 978-1-5326-6715-2
HARDCOVER ISBN: 978-1-5326-6716-9
EBOOK ISBN: 978-1-5326-6717-6

Manufactured in the U.S.A.   JULY 18, 2019

To my dearest wife Helen

Contents

Preface

WE ARE LIVING IN a time of dramatic change in synagogue going. In the Western world, organized religion now attracts only a
fraction of the numbers it attracted a generation ago; in the synagogue, leaders scramble to find drastically new ways of conducting
services in the hope of boosting attendance. This might be a good
time to look back on how Jews (and non-Jews) throughout history
have felt about being in the synagogue, through their own writing.

My involvement in synagogue life began on my eighth birth-
day, when my father took me to join our synagogue choir. Since
that day, I have been a chorister, choir director, cantor and teacher.
Over all the years, I have reflected on the nature of synagogue services, the role of the synagogue and what people expect from it.
More recently, as a member of the historic Kiever Shul in downtown Toronto, I have found myself caught up in passionate discussions about the kind of synagogue the community wants. This
has stimulated me to probe more deeply the question: What does
a synagogue do? From these reflections arose the idea of putting
together a collection of impressions that the synagogue has had on
visitors, Jewish and non-Jewish, over the centuries.

The synagogue fills at least three needs: it is a house of prayer,
a place of study, and a place of meeting. The latter would seem to be
historically the most significant, since the very words "synagogue"
and the Hebrew equivalent *bet knesset* mean exactly that. The association of praying and studying in the same space has given us
the Yiddish word *shul* ("school").

The impulse to write a book about shuls might be in my DNA: my maternal grandfather Israel Isenstein was a bookbinder in Poland, and the son of a bookseller, while my paternal grandfather Siegfried Heller was the židovský rychtář, the head of the Jewish community, in Polná (in what is now the Czech Republic), a position that his own ancestors held in the eighteenth century.

The items in this book consist of extracts from published material or video recordings. They have been shortened by cutting out excessive text; the actual text printed here is unaltered, except for minor adjustments where the original was unclear. Spelling has wherever possible been adjusted to agree with American practice, except in the case of documents in English that have historical interest. Where no translator is acknowledged, the translation has been made by myself.

—Charles Heller
Toronto, 2019

Acknowledgements

In my book *What To Listen For in Jewish Music*, published in 2006, I acknowledged the valuable support received from various libraries. Thirteen years on, many of those libraries have been closed and their books thrown out. It is assumed that for the twenty-first-century reader, the internet has replaced the physical book. The internet can indeed deliver whole libraries to the reader's screen, but there will always be gaps. And so while I regret the demise of the Beth Tzedec Congregation Library and the Toronto Jewish Public Library, there still remain librarians to thank at the following institutions: first and foremost the University of Toronto Robarts Library and its sister institutions the Thomas Fisher Rare Books Library and the Faculty of Music Library; the Metro Toronto Reference Library; and the Pepys Library, Magdalene College, Cambridge.

For productive discussions and helpful direction over many years I thank Rabbis Wayne Allen, Adam Cutler, Baruch Frydman-Kohl, Aaron Levy, Howard Morrison, Geoffrey L. Shisler, Ed Treister, and the late Shulem Langner; and Cantors A. Eliezer Kirshblum, Dr Joseph A. Levine, Benjamin Z. Maissner and Eric Moses.

It is a pleasure to thank the following for generously giving their time to help answer my questions: Dr Tzvika Aviv; Michael Bales; Vince Calabrese; Prof. Adam. S. Cohen, president, the Kiever Shul, Toronto; Josiah Cohen; Dr Jerry Friedman; the late Bernard Glicksman; Prof. Anthony T. Grafton (Princeton University); Prof. Bruce W. Holsinger (University of Virginia); Martin Pavelka; Lila

Sarick, Canadian Jewish News; Prof. Colin Shindler (SOAS, London University); Will Theiss; Michael Wex; Martin C. Winer.

It remains to thank Matt Wimer and Caleb Shupe of Wipf and Stock for their constant support and advice; and *aharon aharon haviv*, my dearest daughter Sarah for her professional advice and encouragement.

All reasonable efforts have been made by the author to trace the copyright holders of material in this book. In the event that the author is contacted by any of the untraceable copyright holders after publication of this book, the author will endeavor to rectify the position accordingly.

The author would like to thank the following for permission to quote extracts from their publications:

Azrieli Foundation, Toronto, for Pinchas Gutter, *Memories in Focus*; Canadian Jewish News; the Cantors Assembly for extracts from the *Journal of Synagogue Music* and *Proceedings*; Ha'aretz; Jerusalem Post; Jewish Chronicle (U.K.); Jewish Renaissance (U.K.) for "Filling the Void"; Prof. Dov Keller, Indiana University/ AHEYM Yiddish Archives for interview with Efim Skobilitskii; Shirley Kumove for *The Zogerin*; the Honorary Officers of the New West End Synagogue, London, for archival material; Penguin Random House for Chaim Grade, *My Mother's Sabbath Days*; Penguin Random House and Penguin Random House Canada for Isabel Vincent, *Bodies and Souls*; Plymouth Hebrew Congregation for the Prayer for the Royal Family; Rabbi Raysh Weiss, for "A League of Their Own"; Robert H. Jackson Center, Jamestown, N.J. for the video *Samuel Adler: Life in Mannheim, Germany*; the Board of Directors, The Song Shul, Toronto for publicity material; The Sunday Times (UK) for *In Search of the Lost Jews of Russia*; University of Nebraska Press for extracts from the Jewish Publication Society of America edition of *The Hebrew Scriptures: A New Translation* (1917).

The Prophets establish the first synagogues

Jeremiah instructs the Jews to conduct prayers in exile

THE YEAR IS 594 BCE. *The Kingdom of Israel has been destroyed by the Assyrians, and all that remains of the Israelite nation is the Kingdom of Judah, now under threat from a new superpower, Babylon. The prophet Jeremiah rejects the extreme nationalists who want to ally with Egypt and fight. Instead, he advises a policy of "keep calm and carry on." He foresees that the entire people of Judah will be exiled, but urges them to keep their beliefs while being model citizens. The concept of a Jewish faith outside the Jewish homeland is established.*

> Thus saith the Lord of hosts, the God of Israel, unto all the captivity, whom I have caused to be carried away captive from Jerusalem unto Babylon: Build ye houses, and dwell in them, and plant gardens, and eat the fruit of them; take ye wives, and beget sons and daughters; and take wives for your sons, and give your daughters to husbands, that they may bear sons and daughters; and multiply ye there, and be not diminished. And seek the peace of the city whither I have caused you to be carried away captive, and pray unto the Lord for it; for in the peace thereof shall ye have peace.

The little sanctuary

GOD TELLS EZEKIEL TO *proclaim to the exiled Jewish people that they will return to their own land. The phrase "I have been to them as a little sanctuary" can also be translated as "I have given them a little sanctuary", meaning a synagogue, which is how the Talmud (Megillah 29a) understands it. The "sanctuary" that is the synagogue has had to replace the "sanctuary" that was the Temple in Jerusalem. The phrase mikdash m'at ("little sanctuary") is now universally used for the word "synagogue".*

> Therefore say: Thus saith the Lord God: Although I have removed them far off among the nations, and although I have scattered them among the countries, yet have I been to them as a little sanctuary in the countries where they are come; therefore say: Thus saith the Lord God: I will even gather you from among the peoples, and assemble you out of the countries where ye have been scattered, and I will give you the land of Israel.

Daniel prays regularly in exile, facing Jerusalem

DANIEL IS IN EXILE in Babylon. King Belshazzar has been slain and a new king, Darius the Mede, has taken power. Government officials petition King Darius to write a decree that anyone who prays to any god or man other than the king will be thrown into the lions' den. Daniel remains steadfast in praying to the God of Israel.

And when Daniel knew that the writing was signed, he went into his house—now his windows were open in his upper chamber toward Jerusalem—and he kneeled upon his knees three times a day, and prayed, and gave thanks before his God, as he did aforetime. Then these men came tumultuously, and found Daniel making petition and supplication before his God . . . and they brought Daniel, and cast him into the den of lions . . . Then the king went to his palace, and passed the night fasting; neither were diversions brought before him; and his sleep fled from him. Then the king arose very early in the morning, and went in haste unto the den of lions. And when he came near unto the den to Daniel, he cried with a pained voice; the king spoke and said to Daniel: "O Daniel, servant of the living God, is thy God, whom thou servest continually, able to deliver thee from the lions?" Then said Daniel unto the king: "O king, live for ever! . . ."

The Jews return to the Land of Israel
Ezra reads the Torah to the people in Jerusalem

AFTER THE FALL OF Babylon to the Persians, the Jews were allowed to return to Judah. Construction of the Second Temple began exactly seventy years after the First Temple had been destroyed. The Persians appointed Nehemiah as Governor, and he facilitated the work of the priest Ezra the Scribe. Ezra instituted the now fundamental practice of regularly reading, teaching and debating the Torah during the synagogue service.

And when the seventh month was come, and the children of Israel were in their cities, all the people gathered themselves together as one man into the broad place that was before the water gate; and they spoke unto Ezra the scribe to bring the book of the Law of Moses, which the Lord had commanded to Israel. And Ezra the priest brought the Law before the congregation ... And he read therein ... from early morning until midday, in the presence of the men and the women, and of those that could understand; and the ears of all the people were attentive unto the book of the Law ...

The Levites caused the people to understand the Law ... they read in the book, in the Law of God, distinctly; and they gave the sense, and caused them to understand the reading. And Nehemiah ... and Ezra the priest the scribe, and the Levites that taught the people, said unto all the people: "This day is holy into the Lord your God; mourn not, nor weep ... for the joy of the Lord is your strength" . . . And all the people went their way to eat, and to drink, and to send portions, and to make great mirth, because they had understood the words that were declared unto them.

Egypt, third century BCE

The oldest synagogue relic

In 1902 a marble plaque was discovered at the site of Schedia, an ancient trading post twenty miles from Alexandria. The Greek inscription commemorates the dedication of a "house of prayer" (proseuche) and is the earliest known synagogue site. The king referred to is Ptolemy III. The phrase "sister and spouse" is a formal title and need not be taken literally.

> IN HONOR OF
> KING PTOLEMY,
> AND QUEEN BERENICE HIS SISTER
> AND HIS SPOUSE,
> AND OF THEIR CHILDREN,
> THIS HOUSE OF PRAYER
> IS DEDICATED
> BY THE JEWS

The synagogue within the Second Temple grounds

Talmud, Sotah 40b

THE SECOND TEMPLE HAD a synagogue situated in its grounds. This passage from the Talmud describes the reading of the Torah on Yom Kippur in the Temple grounds. Some of the details will be familiar to a modern shul goer. The term hazzan *("overseer") corresponds to the modern term* shamash, *translated variously as "synagogue attendant", "beadle", "sexton", or "verger". His job was, and is, to ensure that the services run smoothly. He would also be involved in teaching children and in leading services. The term* hazzan *is now applied to someone with vocal skill whose main job is leading services. The term* rosh haknesset *corresponds to our concept of synagogue president, also known by the Greek equivalent* archisynagogos. *The Talmud is very terse in style and what follows is a paraphrase.*

How does the High Priest read the Torah portion on Yom Kippur? The *hazzan* of the Temple synagogue takes a Torah scroll and gives it to the *rosh haknesset*, who gives it to the deputy High Priest, who gives it to the High Priest. You can learn from this that one may honor ordinary people in the presence of their masters. (But Abaye says, these individuals are all honoring the High Priest.) The High Priest rises from his place in the *ezrat nashim* [the courtyard where both men and women could assemble] and reads three portions. First he reads the portion about the High Priest's ritual [Lev 16] and then quickly rolls the scroll to the portion about the holiness of Yom Kippur [Lev 23]. He then announces: "There is more to be read," and he recites by heart the portion about the Yom Kippur sacrifices [Num 29]. He does not read this third passage from the scroll because it would take a long time to roll the scroll to the correct portion; and Rav Huna bar Yehudah says he does not read it from a second scroll because then people might think there was something wrong with the first scroll. We follow the practice of Rabbi Yitzhak Nappaha: if you use more than one scroll you need a different person to read from each one.

Men and women in the Temple

Talmud, Sukkah 51b

THE TALMUD IS DISCUSSING *a remark in the Mishnah that mentions construction work in the Temple during Sukkot. The issue is that during Sukkot when men came forward with their sacrifices they would mingle with the women, and since Sukkot was the most festive time of the year, things got out of hand . . .*

What was this major construction work? Rabbi Elazar said: As we have learned, the walls around the courtyard were originally smooth, but then they put in projections so that they could erect a balcony round the courtyard. And they instituted that the women would sit up above and the men below.

The Rabbis taught: At first the women would be on the inside of the courtyard and the men on the outside, but they would get frivolous, so they instituted that the women would sit on the outside and the men inside. But they were still frivolous so they instituted that the women would sit above and the men below.

A synagogue dedication plaque in first-century Jerusalem

IN 1914 AN INSCRIPTION stone was found in Jerusalem, dating from before the destruction of the Temple in 70 CE. The stone records, in Greek, the dedication of a synagogue, one of many that existed at that time in Jerusalem.

> Theodotos Vettenos, priest and synagogue president [*archisynagogos*], son of the president, who was also the son of the president, rebuilt the synagogue for reading the Torah and the study of the commandments, as well as the hostel and the chambers and the baths, for lodging needy strangers. The synagogue was founded by his ancestors and the elders and the Simon family.

Rabbi Yosei goes to pray at a ruined synagogue in Jerusalem

Talmud, Berakhot 3a

As THE ROMAN EMPIRE *grew in power, so Jewish life in Israel became more precarious. The centre of Jewish life shifted to Babylon (modern Iraq). Jews spread throughout the empire but some still remained in Israel itself even after the destruction of Jerusalem in the first century CE.*

This Talmudic passage is found in some older prayer books with the instructions that it be recited if one is unable to attend an afternoon service to hear the Kaddish. The point of this passage is that God is delighted that his people praise him even though he has made them suffer. The specific words of praise used in this passage, "May his great name be blessed," form the kernel of the Kaddish, which is recited at every service. Another feature of this passage is the remarkable theological idea that God was forced to make his people suffer against his will, as it were.

It was taught:
Rabbi Yosei said:
Once I was on a journey, and I entered a ruined synagogue, amid the ruins of Jerusalem, to pray. Elijah the prophet (may he be remembered for good!) came and watched over me at the doorway and waited for me. When I had finished my prayers he said to me, "Shalom, Rabbi!" And I answered, "Shalom, my master and

teacher!" He said to me, "My son, why did you enter this ruin?"

"To pray."

"Didn't you pray while traveling?"

"I was afraid that I would be interrupted by other travelers."

"You could have made a short prayer."

I thus learnt three things: one doesn't enter a ruin, one should pray while traveling, and such a prayer can be short . . .

Then Elijah said to me: "What sound did you hear in this ruin?" I said to him, "I heard a heavenly voice cooing like a dove, and it said: 'Oy! Because of the children's sins I have had to destroy my House and burn my Temple and exile my children amongst the nations!'"

He said to me: "I swear on your life and your head that not only does it speak thus at this hour, but three times every single day. And not only that, but when Israel enters its synagogues and schools, and says the response: 'May his great name be blessed', the Holy One, blessed be he, nods in assent and says: 'Happy the king who is praised thus in his house! What can you do—the father has exiled his children! Oy!—the children have been exiled from their father's table!'"

The Roman poet Ovid suggests that if you want to pick up girls, a good place to find them is outside the synagogue

By Ovid's day (beginning of the Common Era) there was already a considerable Jewish community in Rome, made up of released prisoners, slaves, merchants etc. who had come from Judea (Ovid refers to them as "Syrians"). It also attracted converts to Judaism, not all of whom were knowledgeable about their new religion, who would go to the synagogue mainly for social purposes.

Ovid's Ars Amatoria *("The Art of Love") is a guide to dating and romance. In these lines he suggests to the male reader places that would be popular with girls: the Temple of Adonis, and synagogues on the Sabbath—which he advises the reader is not a day for business deals . . .*

Nec te praetereat Veneri ploratus Adonis,
Cultaque Iudaeo septima sacra Syro . . .
Quaque die redeunt, rebus minus apta gerendis,
Culta Palaestino septima festa Syro.

Nor let Adonis, cried over by Venus, escape you, nor the seventh day, holy to the Syrian Jew . . . the recurring holy day observed every seventh day by the Palestinian Syrian, a day not suited for business transactions . . .

Rabbi Eliezer teaches his students how to conduct prayers

Talmud, Berakhot 34a

The Rabbis taught:

It happened that a student rose to lead prayers in the presence of Rabbi Eliezer and he dragged them out too much. The other students complained, "Master! How he drags the prayers out!"

Rabbi Eliezer replied, "He is hardly taking any longer than Moses our Teacher, who prayed for Israel to be forgiven, as it is written [Deut 9:25]: 'And I prostrated myself before the Lord for forty days and forty nights'!"

Then there was another incident when a student rose to lead prayers in the presence of Rabbi Eliezer and he cut them too short. The other students complained, "How he cuts the prayers short!"

Rabbi Eliezer replied, "He is hardly cutting them shorter than Moses our Teacher, who prayed for Miriam to be cured, as it is written [Num 12:13]: 'Lord, please, heal her, please'!"

The synagogue in Alexandria

Talmud, Sukkah 51b

THERE WAS A LARGE *Jewish community in Alexandria at the time of the Greeks and Romans. The main synagogue was so large that people could not hear the cantor, so they needed to see the sexton* (hazzan) *wave a scarf when it was time to respond "Amen".*

The synagogue was destroyed and many Jews killed during the Roman wars, which the Talmud alludes to in its story about Alexander.

It was taught:

Rabbi Yehudah says: One who did not see the colonnades of the synagogue of Alexandria in Egypt never saw the glory of Israel. They said it was like a large basilica, with a colonnade within a colonnade. Sometimes there were 600,000 upon 600,000 in it, double the number of those who departed from Egypt. And in it there were seventy-one golden thrones, corresponding to the seventy-one members of the Great Sanhedrin, each one was made of not less than 21,000 talents of gold. And there was a wooden platform in the center, and the synagogue sexton stood on it with scarves in his hand, and when it was time to respond "Amen" he waved the scarf and all the people answered "Amen" . . .

They did not sit mingled together, but the goldsmiths sat amongst themselves, and the silversmiths sat amongst themselves, and the blacksmiths sat amongst themselves, and the coppersmiths sat amongst themselves, and the weavers sat amongst themselves. And when a poor man entered he would recognize people from his craft and he would turn towards them, and in that way he would make a living for himself and his family . . .

Abaye said, "And all of them were killed by Alexander of Macedon" . . .

What was the reason for this punishment? Because they transgressed the verse that says: "You shall not return that way again [back to Egypt]" (Deut 17:16), and they returned . . .

When he came to the synagogue he found them reading from the scroll the verse "The Lord will bring a nation upon you from afar . . . as the vulture swoops down" (Deut 28:49). He said to himself that since he—that man—had intended to come by ship in ten days, but a wind carried it and the ship came in five days, the verse must refer to him. He fell on them and slaughtered them.

Rabbi Jacob of Paris visits Meron in Galilee, c. 1240

THE JEWS OF PARIS had been subject to such extortions that they had to send emissaries to the East to raise funds. This is part of a letter sent by Rabbi Jacob to Rabbi Yechiel in Paris.

The synagogue of Rabbi Shimon Ben Yohai is a very fine building with an external wall and steps to go down into the cave and many grottoes. It is about two parasangs from there to Kfar Baram, where the tomb of Ovadiah the prophet is, with a great tree upon it which covers the whole length of the monument and near it is the bet midrash, a beautiful building; and there is the tomb of Rabbi Pinchas Ben Yair and near is the tomb of Queen Esther . . . Near there lies a saint who is said to be Nachman Hatufa, but some say it is Rabbi Isaac; and in the middle of the village is Rabbi Shimon Ben Yohai's synagogue, a beautiful building made of large stones and large and long pillars. No man ever saw a building as beautiful as that . . .

Ramban rebuilds a synagogue in Jerusalem, 1267

THE GREAT BIBLE COMMENTATOR Ramban (Nahmanides) lived in Spain and at the age of seventy went to live in the Holy Land. He saw the destruction caused by the Crusades and by the Mongol invasion of 1260—the Mongol Empire, with such legendary leaders as Genghis Khan and Kublai Khan, was the greatest land empire ever known.

Great is the solitude and great the devastation, and, to put it briefly, the more sacred the places, the greater their desolation . . . But even in this destruction it is a blessed land . . . The ten men [making up the minyan] meet, and on Sabbaths they hold the service at their home. But we encouraged them, and we succeeded in finding a vacant house, built on pillars of marble with a beautiful arch. That we took for a synagogue . . . We have sent already to Shechem to fetch some Torah scrolls which had been brought there from Jerusalem on the invasion of the Tartars. Thus they will organize a synagogue and worship there. For continually people crowd into Jerusalem . . . May He who thought us worthy to let us see Jerusalem in her desertion, grant us that we behold her rebuilt and restored . . .

Rabbi Meshullam of Volterra visits Alexandria, 1481

There are in Alexandria about sixty Jewish householders . . . They wear no shoes but sit on the ground and enter the synagogues without shoes . . . There are some Jews who remember that in their time there were about 4000 householders . . . They have two synagogues, one big and the other small, and all the Jews testify that the small one was built by Elijah the Prophet and he used to pray there; and inside there is an ark and near it a chair, and there is always a light burning inside. The synagogue has two beadles . . . They told me that in 1455, on the eve of Yom Kippur, they were left to sleep in the synagogue, they and two others, and behold they all saw at midnight what looked like an old man sitting on the chair, and they determined to go before him humbly and, bowing down, beg something of him, but when they got near and approached him, they looked up and he was no more, for God had taken him. And they told me of many wonders which they had seen in the synagogue. And with my own eyes I saw the twenty four books of the Bible on parchment in four volumes in very large script more beautiful than I have ever seen, and also a scroll of the Torah which Ezra the Scribe had written with his signature, and he left it as a legacy for this synagogue of Elijah the Prophet, and he placed a curse upon the man who would remove it . . .

Rabbi Ovadiah of Bertinoro
travels to Jerusalem, 1487

RABBI OVADIAH WAS ONE of the leading scholars of his time and his commentaries are still essential today. In 1487 he left Italy to settle in Jerusalem, and sent extensive letters back to his family describing his travels. His description of women praying all night on Yom Kippur is echoed in our custom of having extra lights in the synagogue at that time, and reciting the verse "A light is sown for the righteous" (Ps 97:11).

The synagogue at Palermo has not its equal in the whole world; the stone pillars in the outer courtyard are encircled by vines such as I have never before seen . . . You descend by stone steps into another courtyard . . . in which there are large chairs for any who may not wish to enter the synagogue, and a splendid fountain . . . In the center of the synagogue is a wooden platform, the tevah, where the Readers recite their prayers. There are at present five Readers in the community; and on the Sabbath and Festivals they chant the prayers more sweetly than I have ever heard . . .

On the evening of Yom Kippur and Hoshana Rabbah, after the prayers are finished, the two officials open the doors of the Ark and remain there the whole night; women come there in family groups to kiss the Torah scroll and to prostrate themselves before it. They enter at one door and go out by the other, and this continues through the whole night, some coming and others going . . .

In Alexandria there are about twenty-five families and two old synagogues. One is very large and somewhat damaged, the other is smaller. Most pray in the smaller, because it bears the name of the prophet Elijah; and it is said that he once appeared to somebody in the southeast corner, where a light is now kept constantly burning. I have been told that twenty years ago he again appeared to an old man. God alone knows the truth!

Ovadiah reached Jerusalem in the spring of 1488.

I have nowhere seen the daily service conducted in a better manner. The Jews rise an hour or two before daybreak, even on the Sabbath, and recite psalms and other songs of praise till the day dawns. Then they repeat the Kaddish; after which two of the Readers appointed for the purpose chant . . . all the songs of praise which follow with a suitable melody, the Shema Yisrael being read on the appearance of the sun's first rays. The Kohanim repeat the priestly benediction daily, on weekdays as well as on the Sabbaths . . .

Every year Jews come in the Venetian galleys and even in the pilgrim ships, for there is really no safer and shorter way than by these ships. I wish I had known all this while I was still in those parts, I would not then have remained so long on the journey. The galleys perform the voyage from Venice here in forty days at the most . . .

Most of those who come to Jerusalem from foreign countries fall ill, owing to climatic changes and the sudden variations of the wind, now cold, now warm. All possible winds blow in Jerusalem. It is said that every wind before going where it listeth comes to Jerusalem to prostrate itself before the Lord. Blessed be he that knoweth the truth.

The decree of Akbar the Great

AKBAR WAS ONE OF *the Mughal rulers of India. Although nominally a Moslem, he supported all religions and in 1594 he issued this Decree:*

> If any of the infidels choose to build a church,
> or a synagogue,
> or an idol temple,
> or a Parsee tower of silence,
> no one is to hinder him.

Tissard visits the Ferrara Synagogue, 1508

FRANÇOIS TISSARD WAS A French humanist scholar. This is part of his work De Iudaeorum Ritibus Compendium *(On the Rites of the Jews) in which he describes the synagogue in Ferrara, where he studied Hebrew. He is struggling to describe what he sees: for example, he calls a tallit* flammeum, *the red veil worn by a bride. It was presumably not red . . .*

In Ferrara I saw a Pentateuch written a century ago by Parisians, written elegantly, with a pliant quill [*ductili calamo*], and in wide, spacious letters in a large volume. It was most splendidly embellished and placed in their synagogue. And since my guide was an important priest there and a teacher of letters in their school, I wanted very much to enter their synagogue, to see their worship, to hear their singing, and to witness their mysteries. But by God, and by the faith of men! What caves of iniquity they are, what superstition there is in them, what barking there is when they sing the psalms! They have nothing in their temples—or, I should say, their profane places—except benches, stages, books, and a Bible placed in a chest. They light a hundred torches, and each one, covering their head with a flammeum, worships the Bible and venerates it to such an extent that you hear one person barking, another bellowing, and another lowing, while they all sing such cacophonous and discordant things. When I had examined these things carefully, together with their other ceremonies, I almost became ill. But then when I recalled to mind there our own faith, and our ceremonies, and the mysteries of our sacred rituals, I burned with I do not know what spiritual fire, and I was illuminated by divine love, so that I came back all the more fervent in the demonstration of our faith. I marveled at their laziness, their foolishness, their mental obstinacy, and at the pertinacity (which should be eradicated) of those who still wrongly observe the ceremonies of the ancient law, not just in the solemnities of rites, but also in food, and drink, and in so many other innumerable and infinite kinds of superstition . . .

Regulations in the Altneuschul, Prague

THESE ARE EXTRACTS FROM regulations, in Hebrew, drawn up in 1591 by Rabbi Loew ("Maharal", c.1525–1609), subsequently amended in 1745 and again in 1890. They are posted on the wall of the Altneuschul, the "Old-New Synagogue", the oldest synagogue building in Europe still in use.

THESE ARE OLD REGULATIONS OF THE "LION OF THE COMPANY", OUR GREAT AND RENOWNED RABBI MAHARAL (THE MEMORY OF THE RIGH-TEOUS IS A BLESSING) OF PRAGUE

11. On Sabbath after the Haftarah and before Av Hara-hamim the hazzan must commemorate the souls of the holy martyrs as listed in the memorial book.

13. It is a custom in the synagogue that the candela-brum on the south side must be half lit every Monday and Thursday [when the Torah is read], and if there is a circumcision, and on days when Tahanah [supplica-tory prayers] is not recited, it is lit entirely, and also on Festival morning services before Nishmat, and also the candelabrum in front of the Holy Ark is lit entirely on Festival morning services and Purim and Hoshana Rab-bah, and the candelabrum inside the synagogue door. Even for the poorest of the poor, if there is a circumcision the entire candelabrum must be lit, also the candelabrum for circumcision called "The Lamp of Elijah" (may his memory be for a blessing), as it is written: "The mitzvah is accomplished by lighting" [Talmud Shabbat 22b].

14. The candelabrum within the almemar [reading desk] is only lit on days when two Torah scrolls are taken, and also on Purim evening as it is written: "The Jews had light" [Esther 8:16].

19. The shamash appointed to this synagogue will supervise the yortsayts of the holy martyrs, "those who are in the earth" [Ps 16:3], who are listed in the chart, in order to say Kaddish for them, and to light lamps for their souls in Paradise, may their merit stand in good stead for us, Amen.

Rabbi Leone da Modena promotes contemporary synagogue music

From the preface to Salamone de' Rossi's
HaShirim Asher LiShlomo *(1622–3)*

RABBI LEONE DA MODENA *(1571–1648) and Salamone de' Rossi were fortunate to live in the cultural orbit of the court of Mantua in the Po Valley in northern Italy at a time of glittering achievements in the arts. Leone was a poet and scholar, and the author of numerous books.*

Rossi was a colleague of Monteverdi, and his sister was an accomplished opera singer known as Madame Europa. These are extracts from Leone's preface to Rossi's HaShirim Asher LiShlomo *("The Songs of Solomon"), the first ever publication of synagogue music.*

As everybody knows, it is from the Hebrews that the other nations have borrowed music. For who could forget King David, that wonderful poet . . . But our banishment, our dispersal over the earth, the unbelievable persecutions inflicted upon us, caused inevitably the decline and downfall of the arts . . . until this epoch, when Solomon made his appearance, who excelled in the musical science not only among the Israelites but also among the Christians . . . We might say: God has opened the eyes of the blind and unstopped the ears of the deaf . . . Do homage to the Lord by singing this fine music in your sanctuaries on the festivals . . . I am convinced that this work will, from the moment of its appearance, further in

Israel the taste for good music which is well conducted and worthy to praise the Lord.

There will infallibly be people found among us—do not doubt this—who combat all progress . . . I attach here, as an important document, the answer to a question which was put before me when I was Rabbi in Ferrara. My answer, which has been endorsed by all the great Rabbis of Venice, was complete proof that nothing in the Talmud forbids the introduction of choral singing into our temples . . . I invite all our faithful brethren to honor and cultivate song and music in our synagogues, to use and spread them until the anger of the Lord of Israel turns away from us, and until he restores his Temple in Zion, where the Levites will again let their harps and their songs of joy resound . . .

When northern Italy fell to the Habsburgs, Rossi's innovatory synagogue music was forgotten, until interest in it was revived by Samuel Naumbourg in Paris in the nineteenth century.

Mr. Jo. Greenhalgh to his friend
Mr. Thomas Crompton, April 22, 1662

A Visit to the Jewish Synagogue established in London.

THE JEWS WERE EXPELLED *from England in 1290 and were readmitted in 1656, arriving from the Spanish and Portuguese community in Holland and elsewhere. They established a synagogue in Creechurch Lane, at the edge of the City of London (the building was demolished in 1857). The founding community included* conversos *(forced converts to Christianity) who still used Christian terms in their worship, for example referring to the holiday of Purim as "The Fast of St. Esther".*

When it was first opened the synagogue attracted so many curious visitors that it had to give out admission tickets, and eventually was forced to refuse visitors completely. Thomas Crompton was the minister of St Stephen's Chapel, Astley (outside Manchester), but little is known about the writer of this letter.

Mr. Crompton,

When any thing ever occurred in my reading any where concerning the manner of the Jews divine worship (though since the Destruction of their City and Temple) I have always thought it worth the seeing of a Christian; at least for once where it could be obtained . . . But lately having a desire to spend some of my time here in learning the Hebrew tongue, and inquiring of some one that professed to teach it, I lighted upon a learned Jew with a mighty bush beard, a great Rabbi as I found him afterward to be, with whom after once or twice being together, I fell into conference and acquaintance; for he could speak Latin, and some little broken English, having as he told me been two years in London. He said he was an Hebrew of the Hebrews of the Tribe of Levi, and his name (I had liked to have said his Christian name) Samuel Levi. He told me his mother is yet living, and dwelleth at this present in the City of Jerusalem . . . He said he was brought up, and was a student eleven years, in the Jews College in Cracovia the Chief City of Poland, where the Jews have an University . . . and that if I had a desire to see their manner of worship, though they did scarce admit of any, their Synagogue being strictly kept with three doors, one beyond another, yet he would give me such a ticket, as, upon sight thereof, their porter would let me in upon their next Sabbath Day in the morning being Saturday. I made show as though I were indifferent, but inwardly hugged the good hap . . .

I was at first a little abashed to venture alone amongst all them Jews . . . taking off my hat (as instructed) I went in and sate me down amongst them; but Lord (Thoma frater) what a strange, uncouth, foreign, and to me barbarous sight was there, I could have wished Thoma that you had then sate next me, for I saw no living soul, but all covered, hooded, guized, veiled Jews, and my own plain bare self amongst them. The sight would have frightened a novice, and made him to have run out again . . .

The chief Ruler was a very rich merchant, a big, black, fierce, and stern man, to whom I perceive they stand in as reverential an awe as boys to a master: for when any left singing upon their books and talked, or that some were out of tune, he did call aloud with a barbarous thundering voice, and knocked upon the high desk with his fist, that all sounded again . . .

There was brought in a pretty Boy at four years old, a child of some chief Jew, in rich coats, with black feathers in his hat, the priest himself arose and put a veil over the child's hat of pure white silk, fastening it under the hatband that he should not shake it off, and set him upon a seat among the boys; but he soon leaped off, and ran with his veil dangling up and down; once he came and looked at me, wondering perhaps that I had no veil; at length he got the inner door open and went to his mother; for they do not suffer the Women to come into the same room or into the sight of the men: but on the one side of the Synagogue there is a low, long, and narrow latticed window, through which the women, sitting in the next room, do hear; as the boy opened it, I saw some of their wives in their rich silks bedaubed with broad gold lace, with muffs in one hand and books in the other . . .

Each Jew after he had bowed went straight to his box, took a little key out of his pocket, unlocked it, took out his veil and books, then threw his veil over his hat and fitted it on all sides, and so went to his place, and fell a tuning it upon his Hebrew Service Book as hard and loud as he could; for all is sung with a mighty noise from first to last, both of priest and people; saying some prayers; and all was done in the right true Hebrew tongue, as my Rabbi affirmed to me afterwards; which, to this end, they do industriously teach all their children from their infancy, having their schoolmistress on purpose, especially their Service books, which they have at their fingers' end . . . The Priest's son, a comely youth, standing at the Table or Altar alone, sung all the former part of the Service which was a full hour long, all the rest singing with him, with a great and barbarous noise, this consisted mostly of the Psalms of David, with some prayers intermixed, which they sung standing up looking East, and with a lower noise and in tune not unlike to that when the reading Psalms are sung in our quires; but their reading Psalms they sung much what like as we do sing ballads . . .

There was long Supplication, which was the most solemn part of all their service; which they all spake together standing (for they never kneel), with their faces East, often bowing down altogether; it being partly a complaint of the long desolation of their City and Temple, partly a prayer for the coming of Messiah and their Restoration (thank my Rabbi for the interpretation) . . .

I confess that looking earnestly upon them in this, and thoughts coming into my mind of the Wonders which God wrought for their fathers in Egypt, and who heard the Voice of God speak to them out of the midst of the fire on Sinai, and seed of Abraham the friend of God, I was strangely, uncouthly, unaccustomedly moved, and deeply affected; tears stood in my eyes the while, to see those banished Sons of Israel standing in their ancient garb (veiled) but in a strange land, solemnly and carefully looking East toward their own Country . . .

When I was in the Synagogue I counted about or above a hundred right Jews, one proselite amongst them, they were all gentlemen (merchants) I saw not one mechanic person of them; most of them rich in apparel, divers with jewels glittering (for they are the richest jewellers of any) they are all generally black so as they may be distinguished from Spaniards or native Greeks, for the Jews hair hath a deeper tincture of a more perfect raven black, they have a quick piercing eye, and look as if of strong intellectuals; some of them are comely, gallant, proper gentlemen. I knew many of them when I saw them daily upon the Exchange, and the Priest there too, who also is a merchant. It were tedious to relate the several disputes I had with my Rabbi at our being together, and his strange rabbinical and indeed irrational reasonings against Christ. In a word the curse is upon them to the uttermost; and they have a grosser veil over the eye of the soul, than that which covers their heads . . .

Samuel Pepys visits the London synagogue on Simhat Torah, Oct. 14, 1663

SAMUEL PEPYS (1633–1703) WAS a government official under *Charles II, later becoming Chief Secretary to the Admiralty. His* Diary *is a major document from a time of rapid change in England. Pepys had wide-ranging interests, being an accomplished musician as well as one of the first people to own a microscope. He amassed a magnificent library which he meticulously cataloged and housed in glass-fronted bookcases, built to his own design by master carpenters. His profound curiosity about everything around him led him in 1663 to visit the synagogue in Creechurch Lane. (He had actually visited it once before.)*

    Pepys refers to the men's "vayles" (tallitot), the women behind a "lettice" (lattice), and the Torah scrolls in a "press" (ark). Unfortunately, Pepys visited the synagogue on Simhat Torah, a day celebrated with processions, drinking, dancing and general merriment which concludes the solemn cycle of New Year services.

> . . . after dinner my wife and I, by Mr. Rawlinsons conduct, to the Jewish Synagogue—where the men and boys in their Vayles, and the women behind a lettice out of sight; and some things stand up, which I believe is their Law, in a press, to which all coming in do bow; and at the putting on their veils do say something, to which others that hear him do cry Amen, and the party doth kiss his veil. Their service all in a singing way, and in Hebrew. And anon their Laws, that they take out of the press, is carried by several men, four or five, several burthens

in all, and they do relieve one another, or whether it is that everyone desires to have the carrying of it, I cannot tell. Thus they carried it round, round about the room while such a service is singing. And in the end they had a prayer for the King, which they pronounced his name in Portugall [Portuguese]; but the prayer, like the rest, in Hebrew. But Lord, to see the disorder, laughing, sporting, and no attention, but confusion in all their service, more like Brutes then people knowing the true God, would make a man forswear ever seeing them more; and endeed, I never did see so much, or could have imagined there had been any religion in the whole world so absurdly performed as this. Away thence, with my mind strangely disturbed with them, by coach, and set down my wife in Westminster-hall and I to White-hall . . . and so home to supper and to bed.

Dr Burney endures bad singers at the German synagogue, Amsterdam

From The Present State of Music in Germany, The Netherlands, and United Provinces *by Charles Burney (1775)*

DR BURNEY VISITED AMSTERDAM *in 1772 as part of his extensive travels to collect material for his comprehensive study of the history of music.*

As every species of national music seemed to merit my attention, I went to the synagogue of the German Jews, in this city, to hear what the musical performance, during their religious rites, was, and how far it differed from that of other synagogues where I had heard singing in different parts of Europe. At my first entrance, one of the priests was chanting part of the service in a kind of ancient canto fermo, and responses were made by the congregation, in a manner which resembled the hum of bees.

After this, three of the sweet singers of Israel, which, it seems, are famous here, and much attended to by Christians as well as Jews, began singing a kind of jolly modern melody, sometimes in unison, and sometimes in parts, to a kind of tol de rol, instead of words, which, to me, seemed very farcical. One of these voices was a falset, more like the upper part of a bad vox humana stop in an organ, than a natural voice. I remember seeing an advertisement in an English newspaper, of a barber, who undertook to dress hair in such a manner as exactly to resemble a peruque; and this singer might equally boast of having the art, not of singing like a human creature, but of making his voice like a very bad imitation of one. Of much the same kind is the merit of such singers, who, in execution, degrade the voice into a flute or fiddle, forgetting that they should not receive law from instruments, but give instruments law.

The second of these voices was a very vulgar tenor, and the third a baritono. This last imitated, in his accompaniment to the falset, a bad bassoon; sometimes continued one note as a drone base, at others, divided it into triplets, and semiquavers, iterated on the same tone. But though the tone of the falset was very disagreeable, and he forced his voice very frequently in an outrageous manner, yet this man had certainly heard good music and good singing. He had a facility of running divisions, and now and then mixed them with passages of taste, which were far superior to the rest. At the end of each strain, the whole congregation set up such a kind of cry, as a pack of hounds when a fox breaks cover. It was a confused clamour, and riotous noise, more than song or prayer. However, this is a description, not a censure of Hebrew music, in religious ceremonies. It is impossible for me to divine what ideas the Jews themselves annex to this vociferation, I shall, therefore, neither pronounce it to be good or bad in itself, I shall only say, that it is very unlike what we Christians are used to in divine service.

"Delightfull pretty" tunes in Charleston, 1791

GERSHOM COHEN CAME TO *America from Europe and settled in Charleston, South Carolina. This is an extract from a letter to a friend, Mordecai Sheftall in Savannah, Georgia, describing a synagogue service held to raise funds from the Jewish and Christian communities for a nonsectarian orphanage. Cohen's ignorance of English spelling reveals his ear for the spoken language. The Sheftall family were prominent in the Revolutionary War and many of their names are inscribed on a plaque marking the site of the original Jewish cemetery in the center of Savannah.*

Mr. Mordica Sheftall,

Dear Sir:

. . . With a deal of satisfaction, I assure you, I neivour [never] saw more decoram and decent beheavour in a place of worship in my [life?]. The whole was conducted so as to give unive[rsal satisfac]tion. A committe was apointed for that perp[ose . . .] neivour was more decoram observed [in our] synogoge. The hazan and four men and four boys perform all the prayers. The singing was regular (they having practiced for a whole week), and the tunes delightfull pretty. In fact, the performance has occationd [occasioned] honor to our little society and respect to our [Jewish] nation at large. Neivour was aney sett of men so well satisfyed as the Board of Commistioners (say the intendent and City Councle), which they manefested by a vote of thanks to Mr. Azube [Rev Azuby, the hazzan], Mr. Myers [who delivered the

address], and the wardens and elders of the synogoge.
Excuse my inlargien [enlarging] on the subject . . .

. . . bleive me to be, sir,
Your asshured freind and well wisher,
Gershen Cohen

Prayer for the Royal Family, 1762

Plymouth Hebrew Congregation, England

THIS FORM OF PRAYER has been recited regularly in Plymouth, the oldest Ashkenazi synagogue in Britain, since 1762. It is prominently displayed on the synagogue wall, using the wording from the reign of King George V, which is quoted here.

The Lord that giveth victory unto Kings and Dominions unto Princes
whose Kingdom is everlasting,
who deliver'd David his servant from the hurtfull sword,
He that maketh a way in the seas & a path in the mighty waters,
may He be pleas'd to bless, preserve, magnify, extol, & exalt to the highest degree Our Sovereign Lord King George,
Her Gracious Queen Mary,
Alexandra the Queen Mother,
Edward Prince of Wales & all the Royal Family. AMEN.
O Lord King of Kings in thy mercy preserve their precious lives and deliver them from all trouble and danger, AMEN.
O Lord King of Kings of thy goodness we beseech thee to raise and remount the planet and fortune of His said Majesty's Arms, that His enemies may fall under His feet,
and we beseech thee to prolong His days in His kingdom, AMEN.
O Lord King of Kings of thy clemency incline His Royal heart,
as well as the hearts of all His Nobles and Counsellers
to use us kindly, & all our brethren the children of ISRAEL, AMEN.

George Washington's Letter to Congregation Jeshuat Israel, Newport, Rhode Island, 1790

In 1790, Washington visited Newport, and was given letters of congratulation by the president of the synagogue, Moses Seixas. The celebrated phrase "to bigotry gives no sanction, to persecution no assistance" was composed by Seixas, and Washington quoted it in this response. The Newport synagogue, called the Touro Synagogue after its founding cantor, Isaac Touro, was built in 1763 and is the oldest synagogue in the United States.

Part of Washington's letter recalls a passage in a letter sent in 1664 to the newly-formed Jewish community in London by the Privy Council: the Jews could "promise themselves the effects of the same favour as formerly they have had, soe long as they demeane themselves peaceably & quietly with due obedience to his Ma[jes]ties Lawes & without scandall to his Governement".

Gentlemen.

While I receive, with much satisfaction, your Address replete with expressions of affection and esteem, I rejoice in the opportunity of assuring you, that I shall always retain a grateful remembrance of the cordial welcome I experienced in my visit to Newport from all classes of Citizens.

The reflection on the days of difficulty and danger which are past is rendered the more sweet, from a consciousness that they are succeeded by days of uncommon prosperity and security. If we have wisdom to make the best use of the advantages with which we are now favored, we cannot fail, under the just administration of a good Government, to become a great and a happy people.

The Citizens of the United States of America have a right to applaud themselves for having given to mankind examples of an enlarged and liberal policy a policy worthy of imitation. All possess alike liberty of conscience and immunities of citizenship. It is now no more that toleration is spoken of, as if it was by the indulgence of one class of people, that another enjoyed the exercise of their inherent natural rights. For happily the Government of the United States, which gives to bigotry no sanction, to persecution no assistance requires only that they who live under its protection should demean themselves as good citizens, in giving it on all occasions their effectual support.

It would be inconsistent with the frankness of my character not to avow that I am pleased with your favorable opinion of my Administration, and fervent wishes for my felicity. May the Children of the Stock of Abraham, who dwell in this land, continue to merit and enjoy the good will of the other Inhabitants, while everyone shall sit in safety under his own vine and figtree, and there shall be none to make him afraid. May the father of all mercies scatter light and not darkness in our paths, and make us all in our several vocations useful here, and in his own due time and way everlastingly happy.

G. Washington

In Regency London at the porch of the Great Synagogue

From The King Of Schnorrers *by Israel Zangwill*

ISRAEL ZANGWILL (1864–1926) WAS a prominent Anglo-Jewish writer who focused on Jewish and Zionist themes. He famously described the United States as a "melting pot" of immigrants.

In the days when Lord George Gordon became a Jew, and was suspected of insanity; when, out of respect for the prophecies, England denied her Jews every civic right except that of paying taxes; when the Gentleman's Magazine had ill words for the infidel alien . . . in those days, when Tevele Schiff was Rabbi in Israel, and Dr. de Falk, the Master of the Tetragrammaton, saint and Cabbalistic conjuror, flourished in Wellclose Square, and the composer of "The Death of Nelson" was a choir-boy in the Great Synagogue; Joseph Grobstock, pillar of the same, emerged one afternoon into the spring sunshine at the fag-end of the departing stream of worshipers. In his hand was a large canvas bag, and in his eye a twinkle.

There had been a special service of prayer and thanksgiving for the happy restoration of his Majesty's health, and the cantor had interceded tunefully with Providence on behalf of Royal George and "our most amiable Queen, Charlotte. " The congregation was large and fashionable—far more so than when only a heavenly sovereign was concerned—and so the courtyard was thronged with a string of Schnorrers (beggars), awaiting the exit of the audience, much as the vestibule of the opera-house is lined by footmen . . .

When the pack of Schnorrers caught sight of Joseph Grobstock, they fell upon him full-cry, blessing him. He, nothing surprised, brushed pompously through the benedictions, though the twinkle in his eye became a roguish gleam. Outside the iron gates, where the throng was thickest, and where some elegant chariots that had brought worshipers from distant Hackney were preparing to start, he came to a standstill, surrounded by clamoring Schnorrers, and dipped his hand slowly and ceremoniously into the bag. There was a moment of breathless expectation among the beggars, and Joseph Grobstock had a moment of exquisite consciousness of importance, as he stood there swelling in the sunshine . . .

Frances Trollope hears Sulzer in Vienna, 1836

FRANCES TROLLOPE PUBLISHED MANY *volumes describing her travels. Her son was the great Victorian novelist Anthony Trollope.*

Mrs. Trollope was captivated by the singing of the cantor Salomon Sulzer and compares him favorably with John Braham, who was a singer at the Great Synagogue, London, and one of England's most celebrated opera singers. Together with the composer Isaac Nathan, Braham published musical settings of Byron's Hebrew Melodies *which became an international success, partly because the music emphasized a kind of wildness which non-Jewish musicians expected to hear in Jewish music.*

Salomon Sulzer (1804–1890) was the creator of modern cantorial music. He was appointed cantor at the Stadt Tempel (City Temple) in Vienna when it was opened in 1826, celebrated for its modernization of orthodox ritual. Sulzer won international fame for his unique combination of star vocal ability, knowledge of traditional nusah, and skill in composition—his teacher Seyfried had been a pupil of Beethoven. The Stadt Tempel survived the Nazi era because it was located too close to other buildings in the center of Vienna to be set on fire.

There is yet another species of music which I have heard in Vienna, but of this I hardly know how to speak. Were I to attempt expressing to you all it has made me feel, you might, perhaps, think it had charmed away my wits. There is, in truth, so wild and strange an harmony in the songs of the children of Israel as performed in the synagogue in this city, that it would be difficult to render full justice to the splendid excellence of the performance, without falling into the language of enthusiasm. A voice, to which that of Braham in his best days was not superior, performs the solo parts of these extraordinary cantiques; while about a dozen voices more, some of them being boys, fill up the glorious chorus. The volume of vocal sound exceeds any thing of the kind I have ever heard; and being unaccompanied by any instrument, it produces an effect equally singular and delightful.

Some passages in these majestic chaunts are so full of pathos, that the whole history of the nation's captivity rushes upon the memory as we listen; and the eyes fill with tears at the sufferings of God's people in hearing the words "Israel! Israel! Israel!" uttered in the sort of plaintive cry which they introduce with such beautiful effect: but, the moment after, the recollection of their stiff-necked disobedience destroys all sympathy, and almost makes one ashamed of listening even to the words of David from lips which, while they breathe his prophetic songs in strains that seem as if they came direct from heaven, deny the glorious fulfilment of them which has passed before their eyes:—

"Hélas! Ce people ingrat a méprisé sa loi,
La nation chérie a violé sa foi!"

The building in which these people hold their religious meetings is quite modern, and not without some pretensions to elegance. The manner of performing the service is totally unlike that used in the synagogue at Frankfort, and the congregation here call themselves "reformed Jews." I heartily wish for their own sakes, as well as for my ease of conscience while listening to them, that the reform went to something more essential than nodding the head, and rising on tip-toe, which very ludicrous demonstrations of Judaic fervour the congregation of Vienna have altogether abandoned.

Franz Liszt hears Sulzer in Vienna

FRANZ LISZT'S LES ISRAÉLITES comprises 65 pages of incoherent antisemitic rambling. It includes the following passage based on a visit he made to hear Sulzer during a synagogue service:

> Only once did we have an opportunity to glimpse and overhear all that a Judaic art might become if the Israelites might make resplendent, in forms created by their Asiatic genius, all the pomp of their imagination and their dreams . . .
>
> In Vienna we made the acquaintance of the celebrated tenor Sulzer who, in his capacity as synagogue cantor, has made such a distinguished reputation within a circle of true connoisseurs . . . It was in order to hear this that we went to the synagogue where he is the director of music, taking the principal part in it.
>
> Rarely have we been overcome by such vibrant emotion which irresistibly seized all the faculties of compassion and adoration in our soul as on that evening where, by the light of a thousand candles strewn like stars on a vast ceiling, a strange chorus of muted and guttural voices rose up in our presence. Each breast seemed a dungeon from the depths of which an impalpable being darted up to praise, in the misery of slavery, the God of the Ark of the Covenant, crying to him with a resigned and unshakable faith, certain of one day being delivered from this endless captivity, of leaving this hateful ground, these strange rivers, to escape this new Babylon, the great whore, to return to his kingdom in the sight of the terrified nations, in a triumph of unexampled magnificence.

In proportion as the Hebrew words were uttered, one would have said that dark flowers detached themselves from their stems, opening up their vibrant petals, their sonorous corollas, in the air. The harsh sounds, the florid diphthongs, the rough inflections floated and fluttered, grazing the ear, stroking like tongues of flame . . .

No woman was admitted to this sacred enclosure, as if the act of prayer were that of masculine courage and virile force; as if the engagement of this chosen people with its irritable and faithful God, swift and long to punish, slow and late to reward, were beyond the reach of delicate and excitable minds; as if between these men and this God there were a treaty, of which no third party could judge whether or not the terms had been fulfilled. Yet these women included among them powerful souls, like those of Deborah, Judith, Abigail, the mother of the Maccabees; souls full of grace, like those of Rachel, Ruth, Bathsheba, the wife of young Tobias; souls full of grandeur, like those of Hagar, Zipporah, Esther, Hannah the prophetess! Do not power, grace, grandeur, suffice to enter into colloquy with the God of Israel? For that one must be marked with a mysterious sign, the sign of blood!

Suddenly these men, bearing as ever the seal of Abraham bequeathed to the descendants of Isaac and Ishmael, were seized by short, rapid and regular movements, as if providing a rhythm to the eye for their eloquent apostrophes. Soon it made one believe he saw the Psalms soar above us, like spirits of flame; swimming in space, like the hosts of winged cherubim serving as a stepping-stone to the Most High. Jubilant with ecstasy, exulting with celestial intoxication, the majestic stanzas unfolded a tableau of all the powers of the God of Abel and Noah, Melchizedek and Isaiah. It was impossible not to wholeheartedly associate oneself with this great acclamation of the chorus of the circumcised, bearing on its shoulders the burden of so many age-old traditions, so many divine favors, so many rebellions, so many adulterous infidelities, so much repentance, such hard chastisements and such unshakable hope!

Eduard Hanslick hears Sulzer in Vienna, 1866

EDUARD HANSLICK WAS A pioneer in the field of music criticism and music appreciation. He was a staunch advocate of Brahms, and an opponent of Wagner.

"Old Sulzer" is one of the most popular personalities in Vienna. Who does not know him, that remarkable head full of character with locks of grey hair, round fiery eyes and the energetic broad mouth, the beaked nose above it promptly completing the inventory of oriental physiognomy and summing it up eloquently? This man, who a half-century ago, barely seventeen years old, led the congregation of his native city (Hohenems in Vorarlberg) as cantor in prayer, for forty years now has enchanted musical Vienna through the beauty of his voice and the warmth of his performance, still productive in uninterrupted activity, having lost neither his voice nor his youthful fire. Still today as thirty or forty years ago, hardly a foreign musician departs from Vienna without having once heard the famous cantor.

I myself no longer heard Sulzer's voice as it was in its prime; nevertheless his still sonorous baritone and his stirring style of delivery made a deep impression on me. Through this delivery, in which, from the gentlest breath to the most powerful torrent of tones, every note—I might almost say every pause—came from the depths of the heart, the charm of the strangeness combined with an obviously true, warm devotion, he must always irresistibly enthrall and arouse everyone, of any faith or nationality. This was a fire of sound—perhaps a little too fiery and smoky—but in any case the most vivid contrast to chanting ritual formulas with a mechanical, rigid pulse that would be the style prescribed by other religions. A contrite sigh, an inspiring exultation to God, always with the full summoning of feeling, at the same time spurred on by the awareness of representing the whole community, indeed all Israel, in the truth of every single note. Sulzer formerly had a wonderfully complementary and elucidative counterpart in the preacher Mannheimer, since deceased. Old Mannheimer—I still see his gaunt, inspired head with its fluttering hair—preached like Sulzer sang. The same command of the material, the same strange yet enthralling passion which carried everyone away, the same inspiring flash of the eyes and the voice. It was the most glowing oratory in my life, here in words, there in musical tones . . .

As creator and advocate of properly-composed synagogue music he has performed an enduring service, which in visible form, the volume *Shir Zion*, lies open before me. Regarding earlier synagogue music and Sulzer's striking reforms, I cannot be the judge. There is scant information in the literature about the former; I must accept as true and binding the force of the latter. I have found Sulzer's work to be acknowledged by friend and foe. Experts attest that Sulzer has given Jewish liturgical music order, merit and esthetic form, that he has rescued it from a desolate state of caprice and neglect. It is due to Sulzer's influence that congregations which formerly heard the Psalms sung to secular opera and song melodies, with the cantor improvising the most repulsive embellishments, today are moved by well-constructed pieces with musical merit . . .

Rules of the New West End Synagogue choir, London, 1889

THE NEW WEST END *Synagogue in London was opened in 1879, as the Jewish community spread out from its roots in the East End. Home to many prominent families, including that of Herbert Samuel, the first High Commissioner of Palestine, the synagogue has always had distinguished clergy. In the late 19th century its choirmaster was D. M. Davis. With Rabbi F. L. Cohen of the Borough Synagogue, he edited an anthology of synagogue music,* The Voice of Prayer and Praise—*known universally as "The Blue Book"—which is still in use throughout the English-speaking world.*

These Rules are extracts from a small leaflet that was issued to every chorister.

(Historical Note: Prior to 1970, the British pound was divided into twenty shillings (s.), and each shilling divided into twelve pence (d.). Thus 1s. 6d. = 7 1/2 pence in modern currency.)

THE CHORISTER'S PRAYER
May the words of our mouths and the meditations of our hearts be acceptable before Thee, O Lord.

RULES
(These rules were sanctioned by the Committee in the year 1889, and subsequently.)

1. Every Chorister whilst on duty, is actually engaged in the service of God; he must therefore do his best to render the singing as efficient as possible and also by orderly

conduct to make himself worthy of the position which he holds.

. . .

5. All Choristers are to be in their places five minutes prior to the time announced for commencing singing. Choristers arriving more than five minutes late at Service or Rehearsal will be fined as though absent. Absence will only be excused in cases of illness, which must be vouched for by Medical Certificate forwarded to the Choirmaster without delay.

6. Choristers whilst on duty, either at Service or Rehearsal, must not talk or in any way behave unbecomingly, nor may they leave the choir gallery during Service. They must enter and leave the Synagogue in a perfectly orderly manner and without noise.

7. Choristers must not sing in any other Synagogue, without permission previously obtained from the Choirmaster.

8. For breach of any of the foregoing Rules, Choristers are liable to fine or instant dismissal, at the discretion of the Choirmaster. In cases of dismissal, salary is only payable to date of such dismissal, and in aggravated cases all salary from date of last payment is to be forfeited.

9. All engagements are subject to be terminated at three months' notice on either side, dating from such notice, but in cases of failure of voice, (or unpunctuality or indifferent conduct, when Rule 8 is not enforced) the Choirmaster may fix the termination of a Chorister's services and salary for the end of the current quarter.

. . .

11. The following fines are authorized :—

ABSENCE from Service or Rehearsal—an amount based on the Chorister's salary equal to the sum payable for such attendance.

LATE arrival, within five minutes after commencement of Service or Rehearsal—1s. 6d. Any Chorister incurring three fines in one quarter will be liable to instant dismissal.

. . .

The Choristers are hereby informed that well-founded complaints will be considered by the Committee if duly brought before them.

D. M. Davis,
Choirmaster.

Raising funds for the
Great Synagogue, Sydney, 1875

THE GREAT SYNAGOGUE, SYDNEY, was opened in 1878, but it required major fundraising. In 1875 a committee organized a Hebrew Ladies' Bazaar, raising funds by selling donated goods (and charging admission) to a public eager to buy gifts in the weeks before Christmas. The Bazaar occupied a marquee erected on an entire vacant city block; the marquee framework was lent free of charge, and the Sydney Gaslight Company installed lighting free of charge. The Botanic Gardens provided floral decorations, the Army provided a band, and an insurance company donated its security services. Gifts were sent from donors throughout the British Empire, including a cushion worked by the wife of the Archbishop of Canterbury. The Bazaar raised over £4000. Here are extracts from some of the newspaper coverage of the event.

Judging from a private preview, it may be safely said that such a collection of rare and valuable articles was never before seen in Sydney . . . it was a unique and magnificent display . . .

We hear that one of the most sensational sermons preached last Sunday was the vigorous denunciation of the Hebrew Ladies' Bazaar by a Canon of the Church of England, as a work of sacrilegious iniquity which his congregation should utterly shun and eschew at the peril of their souls . . .

More than half of the visitors were, or professed to be Christians: and one evening I noticed two ministers there. One of them was making purchases and between him and a lady of the party, the following conversation ensued:

Lady: "My dear Mr . . . , do you know that every penny you spend will go towards building a Jewish synagogue?"

Minister: "Yes, madam. I think it very likely, unless a great number of people have been 'Jewed' out of their money."

Lady: "But how can you as a Christian minister, whose duty it is to convert Jews and Gentiles to Christianity, actually contribute to funds to build a Jewish synagogue?"

"People who are born into this world," he said, "have a right to live no matter whether they are Jews, Christians or Heathens . . . My wife tells me that these Jewish ladies have given her fair value for her money . . . Thou shalt love thy neighbor as thyself . . ."

From the Rev. Simeon Singer's Address, Rosh Hashanah 1888

The New West End Synagogue, London

REV. SIMEON SINGER WAS *the editor of the* Authorised Prayer Book *in Hebrew and English, which has ever since been known throughout the English-speaking world as "Singer's Prayer Book". His Rosh Hashanah address included remarks directed to poor immigrant Jews who had been given free tickets to attend.*

> I notice in this synagogue a considerable number of our Polish brethren, men and women, who within recent times have left their native land to seek a livelihood in a more hospitable country and I welcome them in the name of the rest of the congregation . . . Remember that, for them, a new life must begin from the moment they touch British soil . . .
>
> You can be of some real use to the State that receives and shelters you. Prove that you are not unthankful for the helping hand that is stretched out to you . . . Get rid as quickly as you can of those unpleasant peculiarities of manners, habits and speech which are said to mark some Jews without distinguishing them, and which are apt to bring shame on all Jews . . .

Sabbath morning in a chevra in London's East End, c.1900

From The Jewish Community *by Beatrice Potter*

THIS EXTRACT IS TAKEN *from a study of the Jewish community that is itself part of a monumental study led by Charles Booth of the working class areas of London, published in several volumes in 1902.*

The East End Jews of the working class rarely attend the larger synagogues (except on the Day of Atonement), and most assuredly they are not seat-holders. For the most part the religious-minded form themselves into associations (Chevras), which combine the functions of a benefit club for death, sickness, and the solemn rites of mourning with that of public worship and the study of the Talmud. Thirty or forty of these Chevras are scattered throughout the Jewish quarters . . . Usually each Chevra is named after the town or district in Russia or Poland from which the majority of its members have emigrated: it is in fact from old associations—from ties of relationship or friendship, or, at least, from the memory of a common home—that the new association springs.

Here, early in the morning, or late at night, the devout members meet to recite the morning or evening prayers, or to decipher the sacred books of the Talmud. And it is a curious and touching sight to enter one of the poorer and more wretched of these places on a Sabbath morning. Probably the one you choose will be situated in a small alley or narrow court, or it may be built out in a back-yard. To reach the entrance you stumble over broken pavement and household debris . . . You enter; the heat and odor convince you that the skylight is not used for ventilation. From behind the trellis of the "ladies' gallery" you see at the far end of the room the richly curtained Ark of the Covenant, wherein are laid, attired in gorgeous vestments, the sacred scrolls of the Law. Slightly elevated on a platform in the midst of the congregation, stands the reader or minister . . . Scarves of white cashmere or silk, softly bordered and fringed, are thrown across the shoulders of the men, and relieve the dusty hue and disguise the Western cut of the clothes they wear. A low, monotonous, but musical-toned recital of Hebrew prayers, each man praying for himself to the God of his fathers, rises from the congregation . . . Add to this rhythmical cadence of numerous voices, the swaying to and fro of the bodies of the worshipers —expressive of the words of personal adoration: "All my bones exclaim, Oh! Lord, who is like unto Thee!"—and you may imagine yourself in a far-off Eastern land. But you are roused from your dreams. Your eye wanders from the men, who form the congregation, to the small body of women who watch behind the trellis. Here, certainly, you have the Western world, in the bright-colored ostrich feathers, large bustles, and tight-fitting coats of cotton velvet or brocaded satinette, At last you step out, stifled by the heat and dazed by the strange contrast of the old-world memories of a majestic religion and the squalid vulgarity of an East End slum.

And, perchance, if it were permissible to stay after Divine service is over, and if you could follow the quick spoken Jüdisch, you would be still more bewildered by these "destitute foreigners", whose condition, according to Mr Arnold White, "resembles that of animals". The women have left . . . the men are gathered together in knots, sharpening their intellects with the ingenious points and subtle logic of the Talmudical argument, refreshing their minds from the rich stores of Talmudical wit, or listening with ready helpfulness to the tale of distress of a new-comer from the foreign home.

These Chevras supply the social and religious needs of some 12,000 to 15,000 foreign Jews . . . Some among the leaders of the Anglo-Jewish community have thought to discourage the spontaneous multiplication of these small bodies, and to erect a large East End synagogue endowed by the charity of the West. I venture to think that wiser counsels have prevailed . . . It is easy to overlook the unseen influence for good of self-creating, self-supporting, and self-governing communities; small enough to generate public opinion and the practical supervision of private morals, and large enough to stimulate charity, worship, and study by communion and example. These and other arguments have led to the federation of minor synagogues and their partial recognition by the communal authorities. And probably it is only a question of time before the East End Chevras are admitted to full representation in the religious organization of the Ashkenazite community in return for a more responsible attitude with regard to the safety and sanitation of the premises they occupy . . .

The Zogerin of Berdichev

OVER THE CENTURIES MORE *and more restrictions came to be placed on women attending the synagogue. By the nineteenth century in eastern Europe, women were accustomed to being seated in such a way that they could not see or hear clearly what was going on, as well as not being allowed to touch the Torah scrolls. In this environment there developed the role of the* zogerin *("speaker"), a literate woman who knew Hebrew and who could explain and conduct the prayers for the other women. In this way the women in the synagogue were virtually conducting a parallel service. What follows is a slightly edited transcription of an interview in Yiddish recorded in 2002 with Efim Skobilitskii, who grew up in Berdichev, Ukraine. (His reminiscences are similar to the experience of my own grandmother Esther Isenstein, who was a zogerin in the Ladies' Gallery of Walford Road Synagogue in North London in the 1930s. She grew up in Brest Litovsk and like Efim's mother in this interview, was the daughter of a rabbi who had a long white beard . . .)*

My mother was a zogerin in the women's shul—the women used to gather in the shul, she used to read from the siddur . . . There used to be twenty shuls in Berdichev before the war [World War II] . . . She was the daughter of a rabbi—my grandfather was a rabbi, the Tchervoner Rav, Nakhman Ben Reb Moshe Kaluzhneh, with this long white beard, a real Jew . . . Tchervone? It's eighteen kilometres from Berdichev, not far . . .

The women's shul? There was a shul, the men prayed below, and the women prayed up above. They used to

wait for my mother. My mother was called Khoneh,
and when Khoneh came they would read . . . She was
an educated woman, in Yiddish—there was a yeshivah
[Jewish school] for men and for women, she went to the
yeshivah, she knew *loshn koydesh* [Hebrew]. In the yeshivah they only spoke Yiddish—Russians also came to
the yeshivah, they spoke Yiddish better than Russian . . .
Years gone by!

Extract from *The Zogerin*

Short story by Rokhl Brokhes
Translated from the Yiddish by Shirley Kumove

ROKHL BROKHES WAS BORN *in Minsk in 1880 and her short story* Yankele *was published to acclaim when she was nineteen. A large-scale project to have her works published by the State Publishing House of Belarus was interrupted by World War II. She perished in the Minsk ghetto in 1945.*

Gnesye the zogerin is a powerful and haunting character. As she pours out her bitterness to her grandson Shmertsik she realizes that her gift for having her prayers answered has been wasted on wealthy, selfish women when it should have been focused on her own needs.

[Reboyne-sheloylem = Master of the Universe
Shabes =Sabbath
Tkhine = prayer of supplication
Reshkhoydesh = Rosh Hodesh, minor festival on the first of the month
Yisker = Yizkor, memorial service]

"No, I say; ENOUGH is enough! On their behalf I prayed, for their benefit I cried my eyes out. Enough! I say, no! May I be struck dumb if I will say one more word, not even my name, Gnesye . . .

"*Reboyne-sheloylem*, kind Father, you alone know how I have prayed both summer and winter, never missed a *Shabes*, never stinted on a *tkhine*. On their behalf what have I not prayed for? Wealth, length of days, pleasure from the children . . . Comes *Reshkhoydesh*, my heart simply melts, my soul leaps. It's no small thing, *Reshkhoydesh*! I pray for everything, everything! Weep for everything! My heart, my heart . . .

"So many women around me, maybe more than twenty . . . the air, stifling . . . the din . . . the bickering and complaining among them—this one doesn't hear, she's sitting too far away, she wants to be closer. Another one is leaning too close to the one beside her. Yet another one thinks that I'm ignoring her, that I failed to remember her grandmother during the *yisker* service. This one, that I forgot about her Khatskele; that one, that I didn't pray for her Iserl . . ."

Her heart was pounding. "Better to fall ill, better to be struck dumb than to have wasted my life praying for fat Teme that she might have such a grand house and so many stores; for Faytl's daughter Shtishe, a rabbi for a son-in-law and such good grandchildren; for that scabrous Tsipore a legacy of ten thousand. For whom have I not prayed and for whose sake have I not pleaded? And what have I gotten from it all? They paid me only a fiver a week and that's *enough*! All they paid me was a pittance to keep my mouth shut. 'Here, choke on it and shut up, for you that's enough.' Can you believe it? . . .

"No, I'll show them. Do you hear, Shmertsik? I'll go on praying, I'll go on weeping but now I'll pray for me, just for me. I'll pray for a disaster to fall on them, on all my enemies . . . they are my worst enemies. They took away my prayers, my tears, my years . . . Do you hear, Shmertsik? All that they have is mine. I'll pray for it back . . ."

Outside the Chesed shel Emess Synagogue, Rio de Janeiro

FROM THE END OF *the 1860s until the outbreak of World War II, thousands of poor Jewish girls, some as young as 13, were shipped from their shtetls in eastern Europe to South America, lured by well-dressed Jewish gentlemen with false promises of marriage or of employment as housemaids. When they arrived they were pimped into a life of prostitution, shuttled between Buenos Aires and Rio de Janeiro.*

Argentina at that time was full of opportunity for men, but there was a desperate shortage of women. In this atmosphere hormone-fuelled men were forced to dance with each other, thus creating the tango, and their only sexual outlet was in the teeming brothels. The local authorities looked the other way, and it was only in such papers as the London Jewish Chronicle *that the subject could be mentioned: "A vile traffic has long been the curse of the city, and many a poor Jewess has been inveigled here by these beasts in human form. The pity is one cannot write in a newspaper of these horrible doings. In a city so permeated with vice it can easily be understood how difficult it is to make headway . . ." The established Jewish community kept away from these women, fearful of encouraging the old antisemitic slur that the white slave traffic had been created by Jews. If a Jewish family inadvertently found itself in proximity to one of the prostitutes, it was immediately shunned by the rest of the Jewish community.*

But one group of Jewish women in Rio de Janeiro had the resilience to create their own synagogue (opened in 1942, since

demolished) and burial society—Chesed shel Emess, "True Charity",
the traditional Hebrew phrase for burial. On the wall of the cemetery, now half hidden by the Brazilian jungle, the women erected a
plaque: "This is in memory of our founders of the Jewish Holy Cemetery and their sisters of the Chesed shel Emess". With its mis-spelt
Yiddish, and its clumsy lettering cut by a stonemason ignorant of the
Hebrew alphabet, this plaque is a heart-breaking witness to the loy-
alty of these women to the Jewish people, despite being rejected by it.
The women were able to persuade a local tailor to act as synagogue
cantor:

> Every Friday night a group of non-Jewish prostitutes
> would gather outside the synagogue to listen to the can-
> tor, whose melodious voice wafted through the red-light
> district at dusk, momentarily rising above the calls of
> the street vendors, the faraway rattle of the trams, and
> the whistle of the trains that sped in and out of nearly
> Central Station. "On their religious days we always heard
> that voice and we stopped to listen because it was so
> beautiful," said an aging Brazilian prostitute. "I never
> understood anything about that religion, about what he
> was singing, but I loved that music . . ."
>
> [Alberto the janitor] escorted the guests to their
> seats in the synagogue, which was on the second floor
> and accessible only though a side door. He also had the
> authority to turn people away, which he did often when
> crowds of young men, some of them Jewish, showed up
> to gawk . . . Alberto politely told the gawkers to leave,
> and when that didn't work he would summon Noah, the
> beefy handyman who lived with his family on the prem-
> ises and was not afraid to use force . . .
>
> One Jewish writer recalled the experience of a friend
> . . . "When he entered, one of the women approached
> him and told him to leave the synagogue immediately,"
> he said. "When my friend asked why, the prostitute told
> him this: 'It is written that when a daughter of Israel steps
> away from the right path the ground all around her is on
> fire. You are now standing on burning ground, sir, and
> you must leave at once.'"

The opening of the South Side Synagogue, Glasgow, 1901

Extracts from the address by the Rev. E.P. Phillips

The South Side Synagogue was the largest synagogue in Scotland. Rev. Phillips was the minister of the historic Garnethill Synagogue which functions to this day. The South Side Synagogue closed in 1974.

Now my brethren, it is our aspiration today to deserve and to perpetuate the splendid encomium which Balaam pronounced on our fathers in the wilderness—"How goodly are thy tents O Jacob, thy Tabernacles O Israel." We must not think that we have fully accomplished our task and duty by the erection of an edifice of noble and imposing dimensions, or rest content with the beauty of its proportions. We know there are some people whose religious ambition goes no further than this, and whose spiritual endeavor and energy are thoroughly exhausted in the acquisition of a beautiful synagogue. Hence it is that some communities never rise beyond moral mediocrity and command little or no influence in the cities where they exist. It should be the aim of every congregation not only to stand well in relation to kindred communities, but also with all non-Jewish bodies with which it is associated by ordinary social, civic, and commercial ties . . .

Unity is the foundation of Judaism and peace is its crown. It is the principle of unity which has rendered our religion indestructible and saved Israel from annihilation. As a nation we need have no fear for the future, no matter how the heathen rage and the nations imagine "vain things" against us. God has spoken on our behalf and His word is our bulwark and rock. But how about our communities and congregations? Are they always united amongst themselves? Does harmony always reign in their midst or concord bless their counsels? Not always, I regret to say. Jealousy, suspicion and opposition are often too strong for gentle peace and unity . . . Interests arise in fierce antagonism, and synagogues are multiplied without reason and utility . . . Communities are killed and congregations are wiped out of existence . . . Much can be done by peaceful and united effort ere this building becomes truly beautiful and acceptable in the eyes of God. There is a "blemish" in its walls which mars its beauty, and so long as that blemish remains, the synagogue will stand forth, not as a House of God, but as a monument of human pride and extravagance. You must make your offering perfect, and remove from it its blemish—the blemish of debt which rests like a huge incubus before the synagogue can be called a House of God and truly consecrated to Divine worship . . . So long as we remain indifferent to its removal so long will our energies be hampered in all directions, our charities, our schools, and all our institutions will suffer and cry aloud unto God against the indifference, the wilfulness, the unjustice and the extravagance which has robbed them of their dues . . .

The Kiever Shul, Toronto: code of behavior

THE KIEVER SHUL WAS founded in downtown Toronto by immigrants from the Ukraine, and continues to hold regular services in its original building, opened in 1927. This Notice, written by a skilled sofer *(Hebrew scribe) in Yiddish, with some Hebrew and English terms mixed in, has been prominently displayed since the shul's earliest days.*

NOTICE
The time of Sabbath morning service is 9:15

REQUEST
We ask you not to wander around the shul during services but to sit down in a seat
Also not to smoke in shul
And not to spit on the floor
And to follow the directions of the Trustees
By order of the President and Committee

The Choral Shul of Moscow
in pre-revolutionary days
As told by Jack Rosse

JACK ROSSE WAS A well-known musician and chorister in London. The Choral Synagogue remained a major focal point of the Jewish community in Moscow throughout the Soviet era and is to this day a Moscow landmark.

I was about eleven when I was auditioned for a place in the Moscow "Choral Shul". The hazzan at the time was Jacob Guzman, who had a brilliant lyrical baritone, with fine diction . . . We were a choir of about twenty-five boys. I was "solo soprano" and there were twenty other sopranos and altos. We were all encouraged to learn an instrument, and I chose the violin, which was to stand me in good stead later in my adult life. The congregation paid for this extra tuition.

It is an extraordinary thing: Moscow, in those days, had a Jewish population of only about 22,000, because of the Decree passed by Grand Duke Sergei in 1896, when Jews could only reside within the "Pale of Settlement"— Russian Poland, Lithuania and White Russia. Jews who wished to live in Moscow, St. Petersburg, or Kiev, had to be of one of two categories: the first was offspring of *Nikolaiski soldat*, men who had served, mostly involuntarily, in the Russian army, from the ages of eight to ten, which endeavored to convert them to the Orthodox Church. Quite a few were converted, being so young, but many managed to stick it out, and remained Jews, and it was the children of these former soldiers who were permitted to live in the capital cities.

The second group were the *perviguldi kupets*, "first-class merchants," in other words rich Jews who could buy the right to live there. Students who graduated from universities were also permitted to remain there.

Because of these restrictions, it was difficult to get good hazzanim and choristers, and we were paid living wages: a hazzan might get a hundred rubles a month, and a leading chorister, such as myself, twenty-five rubles. It was a career for a boy: he could comfortably support his family, at a time when a worker earned six rubles a week.

My parents were separated by this *Ukaz*, this Decree. My father was a learned Talmudist, and lived in my beautiful home-town, Yanova, where there was a yeshivah. My mother, having been married previously to a Nikolaiski soldat, had the right to live in Moscow, where she was the housekeeper to the millionaire Poliakoff. Although Madame Poliakoff was not orthodox, she entertained a great deal, and had two kosher kitchens, one for dairy and one for meat, and my mother was very religious. She earned twenty-five rubles a month, and used to send money home. We had meat more than twice a week, whereas others could only afford it once . . .

I began my career in a place called Liebau, now an important Russian military port. When I wanted to come to Moscow, my mother said, "Mir geyen in shul" [we're going to the synagogue]. Zavel Zilberts was then the choirmaster to Hazzan Guzman, and I requested an audition. I sang the tenor aria *Questa O Quella* from *Rigoletto*, in A Flat. Zilberts said, "You're engaged, I haven't got a voice like yours in my choir" . . .

A male chorister got thirty rubles a month. The choirmaster was also well paid. He had a beautiful flat, nicely furnished, and enough money to buy a good piano and records. Hazzan Guzman used to quarrel with Zilberts, he would shout at him "Galekh!" [Christian priest] because he was clean-shaven. Zilberts was a very good musician: he graduated in composition from the Moscow Conservatory, where Guzman also graduated . . .

Guzman's hazzanut [cantorial knowledge] was elementary, in reality he was more of an opera singer, and gave concerts in the Small Hall of the Conservatory. I used to sing solos and give concerts, especially at Purim time. The choir also sang at weddings and funerals—being children, we liked those! We sang at the synagogue first, and then at the cemetery, which was outside Moscow in a heavily wooded forest. Nearby was a tea-house. We boys would arrive about one hour early and have tea there, and play football during our wait. When the cortège arrived, we sang at the graveside. Of course, these "Jewish Musical Funerals" were for the rich only. When Poliakoff died we had a really good time.

The choir was given six weeks summer holiday. The shul was closed, there was only a little bet midrash left open. Those who wished could go to a datcha, a wooden villa. It was wonderful —it was three days journey from Moscow, and we had kosher food . . .

I was bar mitzvah in Moscow—reading the portion was nothing to me, I had had a good Jewish training. We were all trained, and could read anything. There was little fuss over a bar mitzvah; no kiddush or celebrations. I had no formal schooling: I had private tutors because I couldn't go to school, not being registered as a Moscow resident. I lodged with the porter of the synagogue. The gendarme knew, he patroled our vicinity, and I paid him a few rubles a month. Sometimes they raided Jewish houses, when he would let me know in advance!

The Golem of Prague

THERE ARE MANY WONDERFUL legends about the Golem, the monster made from clay by Rabbi Loew to protect the Jews of the Prague Ghetto. When it ceased to be useful it was rendered lifeless and hidden in the attic of the ancient Altneuschul, the "Old-New Synagogue".

Rabbi Loew ("Maharal", c.1525–1609) was a master of Kabbalah, in an environment where great astrologers and alchemists, encouraged by the Emperor Rudolf II, were laying the grounds of modern science. Legends of the Prague Golem were first published in the early nineteenth century. There had been many golem stories before, going right back to the Talmud, but the stories about the Prague Golem became the most beloved, involving as they did a magician-rabbi, the fantastical atmosphere of the medieval Prague Ghetto, and a superhero created to help the Jews overcome their enemies.

Here are extracts from Gustav Meyrink's The Golem, *published in German in 1915. Meyrink's mother was Jewish, and he worked in Prague, responding to its hallucinatory atmosphere. He keenly sensed the need for an avenging Jewish superhero, living as he did through the times of the Polná Blood Libel of 1899, when Czech Jewry was accused of ritual murder. In this scene the narrator has wandered through subterranean tunnels into a mysterious building and worked his way up a staircase to find a trapdoor in the shape of a six-pointed star . . .*

> . . . I put my shoulder against it and heaved; one second later I was standing in a room flooded with bright

moonlight. It was fairly small and completely empty apart from a pile of rubbish in one corner. There was only one window, and that had strong iron bars. I checked the walls several times, but however carefully I searched I could find no door or other kind of entrance . . .

The pavement on the other side of the street was just in view, but the dazzling moonlight that was shining full in my face formed deep shadows, rendering it impossible for me to make out any details. The street must be part of the Jewish Ghetto, for all the windows of the building opposite were bricked up and merely indicated by ledges projecting from the wall; nowhere else in the city do the houses turn their backs on each other in this odd fashion.

In vain I racked my brains to try to work out what this singular building in which I found myself might be. Could it perhaps be one of the abandoned side-towers of the Greek Church? Or did it somehow form part of the Old-New Synagogue?

The situation was all wrong for that.

Again I looked round the room: not the slightest clue. The walls and ceiling were bare, the whitewash and plaster had long since flaked off and there were neither nails nor holes to suggest the room had ever been inhabited. The floor was ankle-deep in dust, as if no living being had been here for decades . . .

My God! It struck me like a bolt of lightning. Now I knew where I was! A room without an entrance, with only a barred window, the ancient house in Altschulgasse that everyone avoided! Many years ago someone had let himself down by a rope to look in through the window and the rope had broken and. . . . Yes! *I was in the house where the ghostly figure of the Golem disappeared each time!*

Passover eve in the shtetl

From A Page From the Song of Songs *by Sholem Aleichem*

SHOLEM ALEICHEM (1859–1916) IS *the most beloved figure in Yiddish literature, the author of numerous novels and short stories, some of which were used to create the Broadway musical* Fiddler on the Roof. *In this scene, two children, Shimek and his orphaned cousin Buzie, are playing in the late afternoon on Passover eve.*

"The trouble with you is that you don't know what Kabbalah is. If you knew you wouldn't laugh. By means of Kabbalah, if I wanted to, I could bring your mother down here. Yes, I can. And if you begged me very hard I could bring her tonight, riding on a broomstick."

At once she stops laughing. A great cloud crosses her lovely, bright face and it seems to me that the sun has suddenly disappeared and the day is done. I have gone too far. I have wounded her. I am sorry I ever started this. How can I make up to her now? I move closer to her. She turns away from me . . .

Suddenly a voice calls out, "Shimek, Shimek!"

Shimek—that's me. My mother is calling me, to go to the synagogue with my father.

To go with Father to the synagogue on the eve of Passover is one of the pleasures of life. Just to be dressed in perfectly new clothes from head to foot and to show off before one's friends. And the services—the first evening prayer, the first benediction of the holiday season! What delights the Lord has provided for his Jewish children.

"Shimek! Shimek!"

My mother is in a hurry. "I'm coming! I'm coming right away. I just have to tell Buzie something, just one little thing!"

I tell her just one thing. That what I told her was not true . . .

Buzie listens, absorbed in my story. The sun, about to sink, sends its last rays to kiss the earth . . .

I look into her eyes and see in them the last faint reflection of the gold that is draining from the sky.

Slowly the day is going; the first beautiful day of spring is passing away. Like a spent candle, the sun goes down. The noises that we heard all day are dying too. There is hardly a person to be seen in the street. From the windows of the houses there wink the flames of candles lit for Passover eve. A strange, a holy stillness surrounds us, and Buzie and I feel ourselves slowly merging with this stillness.

"Shimek! Shimek!"

This is the third time my mother has called me. As if I didn't know myself that I had to go to the synagogue! I'll stay only another minute, not more than a minute. But Buzie hears her too, pulls her hand out of mine, jumps to her feet, and begins to push me.

"Shimek, your mother is calling you. You'd better go. It's late. Go."

A letter to the *Forverts*, New York, 1909

Dear Mr Editor,

I was born in a small town in Russia, and until I was sixteen I studied in talmud torahs and yeshivahs, but when I came to America I changed quickly. I was influenced by the progressive newspapers, the literature, I developed spiritually and became a freethinker. I meet with free-thinking, progressive people, I feel comfortable in their company and agree with their convictions.

But the nature of my feelings is remarkable. Listen to me: every year when the month of Elul rolls around, when the time of Rosh Hashanah and Yom Kippur approaches, my heart grows heavy and sad. A melancholy descends on me, a longing gnaws at my breast. At that time I cannot rest, I wander about through the streets, lost in thought, depressed.

When I go past a synagogue during these days and hear a cantor chanting the melodies of the prayers, I become very gloomy and my depression is so great that I cannot endure it. My memory goes back to my happy childhood years. I see clearly before me the small town, the fields, the little pond and the woods around it. I recall my childhood friends and our sweet childlike faith. My heart is constricted, and I begin to run like a madman till the tears stream from my eyes and then I become calmer.

These emotions and these moods have become stronger over the years and I decided to go to the synagogue. I went not in order to pray to God but to heal and refresh my aching soul with the cantor's sweet melodies, and this had an unusually good effect on me.

Sitting in the synagogue among *landslayt* [people from home] and listening to the good cantor, I forgot my unhappy weekday life, the dirty shop, my boss, the bloodsucker, and my pale, sick wife and my children. All of my America with its hurry-up life was forgotten . . .

The writer continues by asking for advice on where to go during the Jewish holidays, since his free-thinker friends criticize him for going to a synagogue. Should he organize a concert or a lecture? The editor replies that he should not arrange activities that would upset those going to the synagogue, but should visit friends or go to the library . . .

Yossele Rosenblatt: You ain't heard nothing yet

Yossele Rosenblatt (1882–1933) was arguably the most popular cantor of all time. Beginning his career as a child prodigy in Ukraine, he was admired for his vocal quality and agility, and his gift for melody. The new recording industry made him a global superstar, like his operatic equivalent (and admirer) Enrico Caruso. Rosenblatt's enduring fame was sealed by his appearance in The Jazz Singer *(1927). It is a remarkable fact that this movie, the first talking picture ever made, was about a synagogue cantor.*

These extracts are taken from the biography written by his son Rabbi Samuel Rosenblatt.

> Yossele began to assist his father [the cantor] in the services of the synagogue as a regular member of his choir. The function of the average assistant to the cantor is to sing a few supporting notes, or even solos . . . In this case it was different. Even at the age of four Yossele's alto was of such honey-sweetness, his tones were so clear and the strains of his falsetto resembled so much the trills of a nightingale, that whoever heard him sing was completely entranced. His father therefore permitted him not only to assist, but to chant whole passages of the liturgy . . .
>
> The shul in which the elder Rosenblatt served as baal tefillah was far from being the largest Jewish house of worship in the town of Byelaya Tcherkov with its 10,000 Jews . . . Yet once word got around about Raphael Shalom Rosenblatt's little assistant, the synagogue began to attract a wider clientele. Members of other congregations commenced to attend its services in large numbers, so

that there were Sabbaths and holidays on which crowds of people, unable to get into the house of worship, would be standing in the street outside the synagogue to hear the singing through the open windows . . .

Yossele began touring at the age of eight. When he was nine he visited Lemberg (Lviv):

> The first service attracted an audience of a size unprecedented in the annals of Lemberg. Several hours before the scheduled time of prayer the crowd had already begun to assemble. By the time the principals arrived, it was impossible for them to get into the synagogue, and they had to be hoisted above the heads of the worshipers to gain entry. Inside of the house of prayer people were packed like sardines. There was such jostling and crowding that the doors were battered down and the railing of the bimah was broken. It was a miracle that no one was trampled to death. There were however some casualties. Several of the patrons were injured and a good many lost their shtreimels [fur hats] and the buttons of their coats . . .

Yossele's first position as cantor was in Munkacs (Mukachevo), aged eighteen. He later served in Pressburg (Bratislava), where there had been fifty-six candidates for the position, and Hamburg. In 1912 a Board meeting at the Ohab Zedek Congregation in Harlem, the leading orthodox congregation in New York at that time, voted unanimously to offer him a position.

> The salary of $2400 a year that he was to receive was the highest ever paid by an orthodox congregation in America to a cantor. His side income, he was assured, would at least equal his salary, for it was the custom in the synagogue at the reading of the Torah to make offerings for the cantor. Together with his income from weddings and funerals, this would bring the total of his earnings up to $5000 annually.
>
> After the vote had been taken . . . the chairman, Mr Aaron Garfunkel, a tall dignified gentlemen, the scion of an old American Jewish family of Savannah, Georgia,

arose and said: "Gentlemen, today I feel genuinely proud to be a member of the Ohab Zedek Congregation . . . You have shown how highly you rate the character of Cantor Rosenblatt by the price you are willing to pay him for his truly Jewish rendition of the services of the synagogue, which cannot help having a salutary influence upon all sectors of our community. By your action you have immeasurably raised the prestige of hazzanut [cantorial art] in America. You have given encouragement to synagogue attendance, particularly on the part of the younger and growing generation of American Jews, who will be attracted by Mr Rosenblatt's art."

Franz Rosenzweig among the Polish Jews, 1918

FRANZ ROSENZWEIG (1886–1929) WAS one of the leading philoso-phers of Judaism in the twentieth century. He grew up in Germany in an assimilated family whose experience of Judaism was devoid of religious conviction. As a student he contemplated converting to Christianity but after spending Yom Kippur in an orthodox syna-gogue in Berlin in 1913 he became committed to Judaism.

There are many legends about what actually happened on that fateful Yom Kippur. Some say he was entranced by the fervor of genuine orthodox worship, something he had never experienced be-fore. Or maybe it was the ancient melodies that entranced him. One legend even claims that it was the haunting melody of Kol Nidrei that pulled him towards the synagogue in the first place . . . But it is more likely that he was intending to remain Jewish anyway, and the long orthodox service, with its rich liturgy, gave him an opportunity to focus his thoughts.

During World War I he was stationed in what is now Poland, where he had an opportunity to observe orthodox Jews more closely. Here are extracts from some of his letters home.

> On Saturday I chanced into a Hasidic shtibl [prayer room] . . . the meal came between minhah and maariv, at dusk, the so-called sholoshsudes, "the third meal". The "first" comes Friday evening, and Sabbath lunch is the "second". It was only a token meal, whether because of the war or by custom I don't know; the singing was the main thing; I never heard anything like it. These people don't need an organ, with their surging enthusiasm, the

voices of children and old men blended . . . Nor have I ever heard such praying. I don't believe in all that talk about "decadence"; those who now find all this decadent would have seen nothing but decadence even a hundred and fifty years ago . . .

I told Badt [a friend] about an incident that was witnessed, I believe, by Moltke in the fifties in London. Empress Eugénie was paying a visit to Queen Victoria. A theatrical performance was being given in their honor; they entered the King's box, approached the railing, thanked the audience, and sat down—Victoria without looking round, Eugénie after she had made sure by a glance that there was a chair. Eugénie was probably more of a person than the tedious queen, but only Victoria was a descendant of kings. The east European Jew has his chair behind him and sits down on it without looking around; even the most intellectual of them are more naive than the least intellectual western Jews, whose life-element is tennis, etc. The western Jew always looks round before he dares to sit down . . .

Going to the synagogue in Cairo in the 1930s

Claudia Roden

The synagogue was an important part of our lives. It was a joyous place to meet and socialize.

Every Friday evening and on high holidays, the Grand Temple was packed with people who came to hear Rabbi Nahum's famous speeches in French. By tradition, the prime minister of Egypt always came for the Kol Nidrei prayer. We also attended a small synagogue on top of a garage in the garden of a private house in Zamalek. It was packed with men swaying from side to side (not backwards and forwards, as eastern Europeans do). They sang plaintive nasal chants in Spanish modulations and tunes from Morocco, Syria and Iraq, as well as some copied from the recitations of the Koran and the Egyptian national anthem. Every man started from the beginning of the prayer book, no matter when he arrived, so the result was a cacophony. The room glittered with chandeliers and velvet drapes embroidered with gold and silver thread. The women sat outside in the garden on golden chairs under a pergola. Dressed in colored silk, perfumed and bejeweled, they exchanged the latest gossip about matches, dowries, and infidelities, and visits to saintly tombs. Every so often, a face would appear at the window and shout "Taisez-vous les dames!" ("Shut up, ladies!") and they would stop for a while and intone "Amen!"

Cambridge in the 1930s

THIS IS PART OF a memoir of undergraduate life by Cyril Domb, who became a professor of physics at King's College, London and Bar-Ilan University. David Daube, who is quoted, became a preeminent authority on Roman law.

The present Cambridge synagogue was opened in 1937. Throughout the years it has been maintained by the small community of residents, but in term time the services are largely run by Cambridge University Jewish Society (CUJS) students. The buildings include a kitchen and a dining room, which has always been an important focus of Jewish student life. Dr Raphael Loewe commented that ". . . because catering has come to dominate the use to which the building is put, the synagogue now looks more like one of Pharaoh's store-cities than the Alexandrian synagogue that was one of the wonders of Jewish antiquity . . ." (Dr Loewe's observations on CUJS meals are the subject of a paper published by the Folklore Research Center of the Hebrew University.)

During the vacation when the students were absent there was little Jewish activity. In fact Rosh Hashanah and Yom Kippur nearly always fell at the end of the long [summer] vacation and it was not always easy to put together a minyan. David Daube told me of one occasion on a Yom Kippur when it was felt inadvisable to allow for any break in the service since the minyan might not re-convene! He faced the challenge of a four hour gap between musaf and ne'ilah in which to conduct the minhah service; but, he added, he came from Freiburg, a community whose special pride was piyutim and deliberate prayer; he was delighted to demonstrate publicly that a Freiburger could rise to the occasion. This must surely be a world record for the length of a Yom Kippur minhah.

The character of the community changed dramatically in 1939 with the outbreak of war when a large number of London Jewish evacuees descended on Cambridge. It was of great importance to CUJS that the control of Jewish activities associated with the synagogue should remain in the hands of the students. Among the most eminent of those who settled in Cambridge was the Chief Rabbi, Dr J. H. Hertz, who took up lodgings at the Bull Hotel. The officers of the Society informed him politely but firmly, that whilst they had the greatest respect for his person and his Office, the Cambridge Synagogue was independent and unaffiliated. Dr Hertz took this in good part, and did not interfere with the student organization of the services. However he had no inhibitions about expressing his views on various aspects of the services forthrightly and vigorously. He was particularly peeved with the custom which Herbert Loewe maintained of reading out during Yizkor the complete list of names of deceased members of Cambridge Jewry from the Unnamed Martyr of 1144 up to contemporary times. Hertz expressed his conviction that some of those on the list belonging to the medieval period were not Jews at all, and he persuaded Cecil Roth at Oxford to investigate the matter. He was delighted when the latter produced some positive evidence to support his claim.

Apart from Sabbath services, it remained a struggle to retain people to form a minyan. I witnessed an occasion in the 1960s when the minyan for weekday minhah, held after lunch, was in danger of losing its tenth man. One of the students was a muscular American graduate student researching molecular biology, a subject that was making breathtaking discoveries every day, with at least three Nobelists in the department (two of them Jewish). This student had no hesitation in grabbing the tenth man by the neck and pinning him to the wall for the duration of the (mercifully short) service . . .

Arnold Schoenberg composes
for the synagogue

ARNOLD SCHOENBERG WAS A *giant of twentieth century music. He grew up in an assimilated family and for a period belonged to the Protestant Church—but this did not stop critics from claiming that his challenging music had "the smell of the synagogue". With the rise of Nazism he became deeply committed to Zionism and Judaism.*

Schoenberg's version of Kol Nidre in English was composed at the invitation of Rabbi Jacob Sonderling of Fairfax Temple, Los Angeles, and was first performed on Kol Nidre evening (October 4), 1938. It requires a large choir and orchestra, and so is never performed in the synagogue as part of a service, as intended, in its original version, although a reduction for choir and organ is now available. Here is part of a letter written by Schoenberg to the Jewish composer Paul Dessau in 1941.

> When I first saw the traditional text [of Kol Nidre] I was horrified by the 'traditional' view that all the obligations that have been assumed during the year are supposed to be canceled on the Day of Atonement. Since this view is truly immoral, I consider it false. It is diametrically opposed to the lofty morality of all the Jewish commandments.
>
>   From the very first moment I was convinced . . . that it merely meant that all who had either voluntarily or under pressure made believe to accept the Christian faith (and who were therefore to be excluded from the Jewish community) might, on this Day of Atonement, be

reconciled with their God, and that all oaths (vows) were to be cancelled.

So this does not refer to business men's sharp practice . . .

I chose the [musical] phrases that a number of versions had in common and put them into a reasonable order, One of my main tasks was vitriolizing out the cello-sentimentality of the Bruchs etc. and giving this DECREE the dignity of a law, of an 'edict'. I believe I succeeded in doing so . . .

It is such a pity that people . . . decline to adopt the piece for use in the synagogue, on ritual and musical grounds. I believe it must be tremendously effective both in the synagogue and in the concert-hall . . .

In 1943, Cantor David Putterman of the Park Avenue Synagogue, New York, began a project to commission leading composers to write pieces for the Friday evening service. In an interview in 1976 he remarked: "I felt I had to get these men of great repute to lend their talents to enrich synagogue music". Amongst those invited was Schoenberg, who responded:

It would be a pleasure for me to write such a piece if only I would not have to work so hard, in order to meet the demands of earning money to pay taxes, etc. . . . Please send me the text, in English, since I do not know enough Hebrew . . . How long should this piece be? As you perform 16 pieces in one service, I assume it should not be longer than five minutes. Is that right? Maybe, if the text produces, at once, a good idea which I can carry out in a short time, I might do it . . .

Putterman sent Schoenberg a prayer book in English and received this further response:

The texts you furnished me are much too long and I am inclined to write something closer to our present day's feelings . . . I have succeeded in compiling some words from various places, and in varying them, could produce something which I might compose, if there is no objection from your side. It is still subject to some changes and improvements.

Schoenberg's suggested texts were from Exodus and Psalms and related to the Holocaust and war. Putterman replied that he was only interested in texts that were part of the Friday evening service, and the idea fizzled out. Putterman later remarked:

> I lost an opportunity. I should have said, Yes!! Compose anything you like and we will do it. I didn't have enough sense at the time . . . I lost a classical opportunity . . .

In 1950 the composer and scholar Chemjo Vinaver commissioned Schoenberg to compose a choral work inspired by the traditional Hasidic rendition of Psalm 130. Vinaver sent Schoenberg his own transcription of this music, which he had made in Poland in 1910. Here, Vinaver describes how it was traditionally performed.

> The psalm . . . was chanted by the hasidim during the morning service of Rosh Hashanah. The leader of the prayer *(baal tefillah)* used to exclaim each verse with mystic fervor. The congregation repeated it with the same power and profound emotion—but with minor changes and in a faster tempo. This congregational response shifted key centers frequently, unconsciously creating an atmosphere of unbridled, almost primeval, religious fervor. This mood subsided somewhat toward the beginning of the final two verses . . .

Schoenberg wrote to Vinaver:

> If I could compose this psalm which you sent me, I would be very happy . . . I have a plan for a six voice chorus: Sop., Mezzo Sop., Alto, Tenor, Baritone and Bass. Every voice sometimes singing, sometimes speaking . . . I also profited from the liturgical motif you sent me, in writing approximately a similar expression . . . I plan to make this, together with two other pieces, a donation to Israel . . .

Schoenberg completed this piece in 1950, published as De Profundis Op. 50B, *his last completed work. He died the following year.*

Stop the talking in shul!

THE URGE TO TALK *during services has become proverbial, perhaps because the synagogue is a "house of meeting." Rabbis throughout the centuries have railed against talking during prayers, although worshipers certainly have always observed silence during the* Amidah *("silent/standing prayer") and many westernized congregations even keep silent when they should be responding out loud. Some rabbis thought the endless persecution of the Jews was a punishment for talking during prayer, since they could not explain it otherwise: "Woe to those who talk during prayer, for we have seen many synagogues destroyed on account of this sin".*

Here is a prayer ascribed to the great halakhic authority Tosefot (Rabbi Yom Tov Lipmann Heller, 1579-1654), as printed in a leaflet headed: "Stop the Talking in Shul!" distributed to Toronto synagogues in 2018. The leaflet adds the exhortation: "Keeping quiet in shul is a zechus for parnassah, shidduchim, refuos and yeshuos!" [Keeping quiet in shul will be rewarded with steady income, marriage, healing and salvation.]

> May He who blessed our Fathers Abraham, Isaac and Jacob, Moses and Aaron, David and Solomon, bless everyone who guards his mouth and his tongue, who does not talk during prayer or Torah reading. May the Holy One, blessed be He, keep him from all trouble and distress, and from all plague and illness.
>
> May all the blessings written in the Torah of Moses our Teacher, and in all the books of the Prophets and Writings [in the Bible] descend on him, and may he

merit seeing children living to maturity, and may he rear them to the study of Torah, to the wedding canopy, and to doing good deeds; and may he serve the Lord our God always in truth and integrity, and let us say: Amen.

Tsemakh Atlas reflects on praying in the synagogue

From The Yeshiva *by Chaim Grade*

CHAIM GRADE'S NOVEL THE YESHIVA *centers on the career and conflicts of Rabbi Tsemakh Atlas in Lithuania before World War II. Although fiction, Chaim Grade is describing vividly the world he grew up in.*

He stepped behind the porch for a moment, eyes closed, wanting to blend with the stillness of the night . . . He felt drawn to the homely warmth of a bet midrash full of Jews. On Friday night the electric lamps and the lit candles on the lectern flamed with a tremulous gold that was completely different from the light of midweek; but the heavens did not change, the stars in the sky did not shine any differently in honor of the Sabbath . . . In our holy place of worship the quiet joy of praying glowed on everyone's face—on the scholar's and on the rich man's by the eastern wall, as well as on the pauper's and on the common workman's sitting behind the pulpit. Praying revealed something dormant within everyone. It manifested itself clearly after a secret life deep within, as if the worshiper had shouted down into a deep well and heard his bizarre echo resounding from the depths. If the worshiper was a man of heightened piety, the prayer overwhelmed his body and spirit, his life and soul. All his limbs trembled with ecstatic joy. But even when the worshiper was a simple sort who prayed for health and livelihood, for his wife and children—such a man derived joy from the prayer itself. After the service he felt purified, like the sky cleared of rain clouds.

Things get out of hand in the Valkenik Bet Midrash

From The Yeshiva *by Chaim Grade*

On a hot summer *Sabbath, different political factions clash in the synagogue. Lithuanian Jews before World War II comprised the very orthodox, the Zionists (the Mizrachi party), secularists, socialists, and all shades in between. In this scene from the novel, tensions rise as Dan Dunietz, a guest of the modernists, tries to persuade the synagogue to broaden their library to include Western thought. Problems arise when the Haftarah is read. This particular Sabbath is the Sabbath of Consolation, when the words of Isaiah "Comfort ye my people" are read. The honor of reading is supposed to go to Reb Eltzik, the Mizrachi leader, but in a last-minute switch it goes to his anti-Zionist brother-in-law Reb Hirshe Gordon, on the pretext that he was commemorating the yortsayt of a deceased grandfather (or great-grandfather).*

At that moment the library supporters marched in and, standing shoulder to shoulder, approached the Holy Ark as if taking up battle positions . . . The worshipers turned to the pulpit, curious to see how Reb Hirshe would handle the situation. To their amazement Reb Hirshe winked to the cantor not to take the Torah back to the Ark just yet. If these apostates want to talk, let them talk.

Dan Dunietz went up to the steps of the Holy Ark and began, "The Midrash says . . ."

Reb Hershe Gordon had previously arranged with his supporters that the heretics should be allowed to say what they had to say and then the congregation could continue with the musaf prayers undisturbed. And when the time came to provide money for books, they'd be put in their places. But Reb Hirshe had not expected Dunietz to have the gall to begin with a verse from the Midrash. The blood rushed to his temples; his face turned red.

"You're quoting the sages? First show me your fringes! Let me see that you have on ritual fringes like me and everyone else in this bet midrash . . ."

Dan Dunietz was bewildered . . . Mayerke Podval from Panashishok answered for him. "And are ritual fringes obligatory if one is wearing a tallis?"

"Whether they are or not, you're a Bolshevik and a convicted jailbird. You shouldn't have lived to get out of prison!" Reb Hirshe screamed. He pointed at Dan Dunietz. "Get him out of here!"

Sroleyzer the bricklayer and his gang of helpers suddenly materialized by the Holy Ark . . . "We're not asking Reb Hirshe's opinion. He's not a member of the community council."

But Gordon was now ranting at the highest pitch: "Drag that rebel down from there!" And his side chimed in, "Get him down, down!"

Dan Dunietz had recovered by now . . . "Those liars! . . . They prefer the Exile in Valkenik, their Valkenik Diaspora, over the return to Zion."

But Dan Dunietz got no further. Hands stretched out to grab him, and in a flash he was flying down the steps. One of the town crooks jabbed five hard fingers into the cheek of the intellectual Moshe Okun. "You half-dead corpse! Who are you shoving?"

"I protest," Moshe Okun answered softly and, clawing with all his fingers, he bloodied the crook's face . . .

The fight spread . . . A knee in the belly, a fist in the chest, a head butt to the chin. The library crowd returned the blows with blind fury, almost foaming at the mouth. They attacked with prayer stands and smacked heads with heavy Talmuds; they swung their elbows and kicked left and right. They were out for blood . . .

Other congregants shouted: "A plague on both your houses! Every Sabbath there's another to-do in the shul

. . . We have to eat stone-cold cholent because of these delays in the services . . ."

During all this the old ritual slaughterer Reb Lippa-Yosse was banging on the prayer stand and screaming with all his might, "You bastards! You're desecrating the Sabbath . . ."

Incidents at the Western or Wailing Wall in Jerusalem, 1928

Memorandum by the Secretary of State for the [British] Colonies, Presented to Parliament by Command of His Majesty, 1928

On the evening of the 23rd September, the eve of the Day of Atonement, a complaint was made to the Deputy District Commissioner, Jerusalem, by the Mutawali of the Abu Madian Waqf, in which the pavement and the whole area around the Western or Wailing Wall is vested, to the effect that a dividing screen had been affixed to the pavement adjoining the Wall, and that other innovations had been made in the established practice, such as the introduction of additional petrol lamps, a number of mats, and a tabernacle or ark much larger than was customary . . . The Deputy District Commissioner gave instructions to the beadle in charge . . . The beadle undertook to remove the screen and the Deputy District Commissioner gave him until early the following morning to do so . . . at the same time informing the British Police Officer on duty that in the event of the beadle not complying with his undertaking the screen was to be removed.

On the following morning the Police Officer visited the Wall and, finding that the screen had not been removed, asked members of the congregation present to take it away; they replied that they were unable to move it because of the holiness of the day. The Police therefore removed the screen themselves. The worshippers in general, unaware of the circumstances that had gone before and seeing only the Police in the act of removing the screen which had been used to separate the men and the women, became excited and some of them endeavoured by force to prevent the screen being taken away. Ultimately the screen was removed.

The importation of the screen and its attachment to the pavement constituted an infraction of the status quo, which the Government were unable to permit. At the same time the Government deeply deplore the shock that was caused to large numbers of religious people on a day so holy to Jews. Government . . . have impressed on the Jewish authorities the need, manifested in connexion with the incidents at the Wall in 1922 and 1925 and again on this occasion, for prior consultation with the proper officers of Government as to the arrangements for the services . . . Government will, however, consider the desirability of a responsible Jewish Officer being included in future among the officers detailed for duty at the Wall on solemn Jewish holy days . . .

The Palestine Government and His Majesty's Government, having in mind the terms of Article 13 of the Mandate for Palestine, have taken the view that the matter is one in which they are bound to maintain the status quo, which they have regarded as being, in general terms, that the Jewish community have a right of access to the pavement for the purposes of their devotions, but may bring to the Wall only those appurtenances of worship which were permitted under the Turkish régime . . . The conclusion of both the Permanent Mandates Commission and the Council of the League of Nations was that a solution of the difficulties could only be found by agreement, thus endorsing the comment of His Majesty's Government . . . that the dispute could not be settled except by common consent . . . Government is not aware of any negotiations having been initiated between the parties . . .

At the Western Wall, 1930

Report of the Commission appointed by His Majesty's Government in the United Kingdom of Great Britain and Northern Ireland, with the approval of the Council of the League of Nations, to determine the rights and claims of Moslems and Jews in connection with the Western or Wailing Wall at Jerusalem, 1930

The International Commission for the Wailing Wall has the honour to submit the following report to His Britannic Majesty's Government . . .

It ought to be mentioned that the Commissioners—although the mandate entrusted to them did not explicitly refer to conciliation—thought it a duty incumbent upon them to try to bring about a friendly settlement between the Parties . . . After the Commission had left Palestine, the negotiations between the parties were continued in the presence of representatives of the Palestine Government . . . It is with great regret that the Commission has had to ascertain the failure, up to the present time, of the said negotiations . . .

The Jewish Side claim that, according to Article 15 of the Mandate, the Mandatory Power shall guarantee the Jews free exercise of worship at the Wall in the form prescribed by the ritual of their religion without any interference whatever from the Arabs or the adherents of any other religion. Still more, the Arabs should be prohibited from disturbing the Jewish services by leading donkeys through the passage or by installing a muezzin in the neighbourhood of the Wall or by conducting the Zikhr ritual in the courtyard at the southern end of the Pavement, to which the Jews object because of the concomitant disagreeable noise . . .

The contentious problem that the Commission has had to deal with . . . has arisen out of an existing incompatibility in actual principles of right and religious faith . . .

It is fitting here to recall the fact that, in the Treaty between the European Great Powers and Turkey for the settlement of the affairs of the East, signed on 13th July, 1878, the Sublime Porte made a spontaneous declaration, in which there was expressed the intention to maintain the principle of religious liberty and to give it the widest scope (Article LXII).

In regard to the particular case that the Commission has been appointed to inquire into, this lofty principle cannot be put into practice, unless the adherents of the differing creeds are prepared . . . to show each other due consideration—as regards the one Party in the exercise of their incontestable rights of ownership and possession, and as regards the other in the performance of their religious services on a ground which does not belong to them by right of possession.

The Commission ventures to entertain the hope that . . . both Moslems and Jews will accept and respect the Commission's Verdict with that earnest desire to attain mutual understanding that is so important a pre-requisite both for the furtherance of the common interest of the Parties in Palestine and for ensuring a peaceable development in the World at large.

Kristallnacht at the
Mannheim Central Synagogue

SAMUEL ADLER IS A distinguished composer and former member of the faculty of the University of Rochester Eastman School of Music. He is the son of composer and cantor Hugo Chaim Adler. This is a slightly edited transcript of an interview he gave in 2006.

On the night of 9 November, 1938, the Nazis attacked Jews and destroyed synagogues and Jewish property throughout Germany and Austria. That night became known as Kristallnacht—*the night of broken glass.*

Here's what happened on Kristallnacht.

At two o'clock in the morning of the 9th–10th November, 1938, we heard a big explosion. We lived outside the center of the city of Mannheim and we heard this explosion—it was the chapel of the Jewish cemetery. My father was the chief cantor at the Central Synagogue, so he didn't usually conduct ordinary morning services on weekdays except Rosh Hodesh, the first of the month [on the Jewish calendar], a sort of holiday. It was the first of the month, and so he had to do services at six in the morning. He always rode his bicycle into town so he saw the cemetery in flames. Somebody recognized him and said, "You've got to get him!" But he escaped and came home and said, "We have to get our passports . . ."

My father had always hated the synagogue music that had been used for hundreds of years. There was a big choir and a big organ. They tried to destroy the Central Synagogue but it was right in the middle of a block of apartments. They couldn't put a firebomb in it but they put an explosive charge into the Ark and blew that out, and also under the organ. My father said to my mother, "We've got to rescue the music of the Mannheim Synagogue!"

She said, "You're crazy, there are SS men in the building!"

My father said, "I'm going to take Sam and we're going to go up to the choir loft."

Well, my father always got his way. The SS were patrolling the ruins, but he knew a way to get into the synagogue without being spotted, underneath the street and upstairs to the choir loft. You've never seen such a disaster—there was a big hole where the organ had been, and the organ was now hanging by a single cable over the gallery. Well, we did get the music—there were seventeen part-books, they were all over the place, but we did get them. We were just about to go down, but there was so much dust that I sneezed. The SS captain downstairs heard me, and gave an order: "Go upstairs and shoot at sight!"

At that moment the organ fell down.

So I'm here.

The last minyan in Germany, 1938

AFTER KRISTALLNACHT, ALL SYNAGOGUES in Germany were closed. But the Real-gymnasium *[High School] of the Adath Yisrael in Berlin had survived the destruction, and the students continued to organize their usual daily services, held in a large schoolroom. The school's principals, Max Sinasohn and Dr Nachman Schlesinger, convinced the Gestapo that, as they were a school, their regular minyan could not be considered a "Jewish house of worship", and so was allowed to continue, albeit with stringent conditions. This is part of a memoir by one of the schoolboy organizers, Emil Lowenstein, who fled to Britain.*

For some two weeks, ours was the only officially open synagogue in Germany, and Raphael Levy and I the only officially accredited and authorized wardens. But, of course, it was not that simple. The conditions stipulated that only the usual room could be used, that only pupils could conduct services, and that two uniformed SS men were to be present throughout.

The news that our minyan was open spread like wildfire across Berlin, and especially on the two Shabbatot many hundreds came to us from all over the city. There were dozens of bar mitzvah boys, bridegrooms and Yahrzeits, not to mention rabbis and a multitude of ordinary Jews who wanted to pour out their hearts to the Almighty at this terrible time.

The SS men would allow no adults to be called to the Torah, but we were able to smuggle in a few of the bar mitzvah boys. The overcrowded congregation was addressed by Sinasohn and Schlesinger, who tried hard to keep up our spirits without offending the SS.

The atmosphere was electric. Many a tear was shed and we all sensed that this was a unique moment in our history, a true Kiddush Hashem. Though no one could foresee the future, there was foreboding and apprehension, as well as fervent hope, and prayer was rarely more meaningful than during those services.

The Nuremberg laws prohibited more than three Jews standing or walking together (lest they become a "riotous assembly") and so, after the service, Levy and I were charged by the Gestapo to ensure that this rule was strictly obeyed. Worshipers had to cross the large courtyard and it took five hours until everyone had left and we ourselves could go home.

Seven months later, the school was closed and the building was taken over by the Air Ministry and, eventually, by the Hitler Youth.

Sinasohn survived . . . Schlesinger and his large family perished in a Nazi extermination camp—as, no doubt, did many (if not most) of those who worshiped with us during that fateful fortnight.

Bar mitzvah in the Czestochowa
Labor Camp, Poland, 1944

PINCHAS GUTTER GREW UP *in Lodz, Poland, and was seven when World War II began. He survived the Warsaw Ghetto, Majdanek and Buchenwald, and after working and traveling throughout the world settled in Toronto. He is much sought after as a witness to the Holocaust and for his message: "All I want is to impart a true picture, construct a tapestry of what has already happened, what can happen again and what shouldn't happen, if possible. I want to offer some kind of hope to people who are suffering injustice and tell them that one can outlive the evil and build a new life."*

Another Holocaust survivor now living in Toronto, John Freund, remarked in an interview on CBC Radio: "My survival was due 98% to luck and 2% to strength, willpower and the moral teachings of my parents."

When I arrived at the camp, I found Rav Godel Eisner, a great Talmudist who had been a friend of my father's since they had studied in the same yeshivah together. One day, Rav Eisner came to me and said, " I was at your brit milah [circumcision], and now that you are turning thirteen, we're going to make you a bar mitzvah." By that time I had lost all hope and long neglected any religious observances. I didn't want to go through with it and was afraid of the possible consequences. Even though this camp was more flexible and not so strict, it was an extremely dangerous undertaking. There were constant *Appells* [roll calls] and we were closely watched. No matter how kind some of the guards might be, we knew we were risking death. Besides, I felt no religious need for it; I told Rabbi Eisner that I didn't want a bar mitzvah, and I began avoiding him from that day on. I tried to keep out of his way but he persisted until I finally agreed.

Rav Eisner was not in my barracks so on the night we arranged for the bar mitzvah, I exchanged places with a person from his barracks—he came to sleep in my bunk right before curfew and I went to his barracks for my bar mitzvah. I hid under his bunk until all was quiet and then we proceeded quickly. Even though any type of religious observance was strictly forbidden in the camps, religious Jews managed to find ways to continue to practise their faith. I don't know how, but they managed to smuggle all kinds of things in; Rav Eisner had managed to smuggle *tefillin*, the black leather box and straps that Jewish men wear to pray, and a siddur, the Jewish prayer book. He put on the *tefillin* and gathered ten men for a minyan. I repeated the *brakhot*, the benedictions, after him and then the minyan prayed together. When he was done, he *bentshed* [blessed] me, and said a few times in Yiddish, *"Mit gots hilf vest du iberlebn Hitler."* (With God's help, you will survive Hitler.)

In spite of myself, I was caught up in the fervor of the event and it renewed my hope that I might actually, with God's help, survive . . . It gave me strength.

Pinchas was later sent to Buchenwald and then Colditz, where he was assigned to the kitchen, which enabled him to regain his strength:

It just so happened that Rav Godel Eisner had also been sent to Colditz, and we met there again . . . So, in the evenings, after I had eaten my fill in the kitchen, I would give Rav Eisner my ration of bread and soup . . . That's how it works, God's Providence. The Rav made my bar mitzvah in a dangerous and unlikely place and when I found him later, I was able to give him some extra food to help him stay alive . . .

The ruined synagogues of post-war Vilna

From My Mother's Sabbath Days *by Chaim Grade*

CHAIM GRADE GREW UP in Vilna [Vilnius], Lithuania, and survived World War II by escaping to remote parts of the Soviet Union, leaving his family behind. After the war he returned to Vilna, only to discover that his wife and his family had perished. In these extracts from his memoir, he spends Yom Kippur searching for the familiar synagogues of his youth, and recalls how services were conducted by the sexton and slaughterer Reb Dov-Ber, who on Yom Kippur would stand on the bimah and in a melodic chant auction off the honor of opening the Ark.

There it is—Reb Shaulka's Synagogue! I lunge fiercely at the boarded-up door, which emits a muffled groan, like a wooden gallows when the corpse is cut down. In the death-emptied Ghetto the silence reverberates, as though the ruins are shuddering at my desecration of the Day of Atonement. With murderous force I continue pulling at the door, until at last the rotted boards give way. I go up into the bet midrash—it is in ruins, as in all the other synagogues. But on the wall, in the southwest corner, there still hangs a tablet whose inscription I remember from childhood: "The woman Lieba, daughter of Reb Azriel Hellin, has bequeathed three thousand rubles . . ."

"Twenty gulden for the Opening of the Ark . . ."

Reb Dov-Ber looks around: Who will bid more? A congregant at the east wall raises a finger; the sexton understands the signal and calls out:

"Twenty-five gulden for the Opening of the Ark . . ."

The first bidder now blazes up, and raises his whole hand. The sexton continues his chant:

"Thirty gulden for the Opening of the Ark . . ."

I stare at the bimah and a gasp, a wailing, bursts from my throat, as though someone were strangling me:

"Twenty thousand Jews for the Opening of the Ark. But the Gate of Heaven did not open . . .

"Forty thousand Jews for the Opening of the Ark. But the Gate of Mercy remained locked . . .

"Seventy thousand Jews have perished. Communities outbid each other: Which would bring more sacrifices? But none could induce the Gate of Mercy to open. Reb Ber, pound the desk: Enough of sacrifices! . . ."

The bet midrash is empty, silent. I descend the steps . . .

Another synagogue!

This is the small house on Szawelska Street where poor workingmen came to pray and weary shopkeepers would rush in to recite Kaddish . . . I drag myself up . . . and abruptly halt, overcome with amazement.

Out of the buckled floor has sprouted an entire field of sunflowers. Their leafy yellow heads tower over me, they radiate a golden brightness like that of a thousand suns revolving around one another. They tremble in such joyful ecstasy that one might think them the poverty-stricken congregants of the synagogue, gloriously transformed. They nod their heads toward the empty Ark, as if the open repository were still filled with sacred scrolls . . . It is with careful, quiet steps that I descend the stairs, so as not to disturb the silent devotions of these luminous flowers.

Once outside, I hurry quickly away: I need to see how the setting sun of Ne'ilah shines upon the spiderwebs in my mother's doorway . . .

Those are not spiderwebs, my little Mother, hanging in your doorway, but a curtain of gold for the Holy Ark, and behind it a Holy of Holies. In the Holy of Holies in the Temple, the Divine Presence hovered between two cherubim, and in your home the Divine Presence hovered every Friday night between two poor Sabbath candles in their copper candlesticks . . . Now, my little Mother, the glow of your ten-groschen Sabbath candles has been woven into a sunny, golden curtain for the Holy Ark, and it hangs before your door.

The destruction of the Great Synagogue, London

THE GREAT SYNAGOGUE IN London's East End was opened in 1722. It was destroyed by fire during the Blitz in 1941, recalled in an article by Frank Rose, the son of the last head beadle.

Although the pre-war congregation consisted typically of a cross-section of local residents, plus a sprinkling of visitors, the standards the Great Synagogue set itself and strictly adhered to under the guidance of a strong and charismatic warden, Dr Israel Feldman, continued to reflect the values of a sophisticated but mainly absent Anglo-Jewish establishment.

So at root, perhaps, for most people there was the sense of sheer contrast between hard and precarious everyday reality, with its tenement blocks, workshops, market stalls, and this polished other-world on their doorsteps, with its dignified order and gracious decorum tempered by twinkling eyes and nodding heads.

The reputation of the Great Synagogue to create a sense of occasion—or simply to enchant—was probably unmatched anywhere in the English-speaking world . . . The place would gleam with silk hats and candle lamp. Uniformed beadles would hover like school prefects. Nothing was ever expected to go wrong . . .

We occupied a third-floor private flat on the premises and I grew up in the shul . . . When the crowds had gone, there the synagogue remained, a repository of childhood fantasies and emotions, heavy with shadows and foreboding in the twilight of dimly-lit Sabbath afternoons, empty and yellow with sunlight when, from the pulpit, I addressed vast silent congregations.

But when the crowds returned at weekends the building became alive. Those Friday-evening services with the guest preachers and the music of Samuel Alman became famous . . .

One of the highlights of the Sabbath-morning service was the dramatic rendering [by the cantor, Simcha Kusevitsky] of the prayer which follows the return of the Torah scroll to the Ark. Gathering momentum, he would either storm the synagogue on the final word *k'kedem* with a commanding top note in full voice, or he would drop on the last syllable to a lower octave. We used to wait on tenterhooks, hoping—but my father, who stood beside him, was fearful for his sake, and one day told him so. Whether this influenced him or not I do not know, but increasingly we had to be content with the more moderate conclusion . . .

That world has disappeared, those days cannot be renewed as of old. On the morning of May 11, 1941, when the all-clear sounded after one of London's heaviest air raids, the Great Synagogue stood unscathed: ironically, it had survived the Blitz.

Later in the morning, exhausted firemen, handicapped by the shortage of water, stood by helpless as the conflagration spread from an adjacent block. In those last moments my father opened the Ark and carried the scrolls to safety—his final service to the old Great Synagogue.

Prince Philip at Bevis Marks, London

By a Jewish Chronicle Reporter, December 21, 1951

In the presence of H.R.H. The Duke of Edinburgh eight hundred worshipers at the Bevis Marks Synagogue on Wednesday attended a service to mark the synagogue's 250th anniversary. This was the first royal visit to Bevis Marks, the oldest existing synagogue in Britain, a fact which lent important evidence to the rich dignity of the occasion. The Duke occupied the seat of Sir Moses Montefiore . . . The Duke followed the service from a specially bound prayer-book, and the order of prayer was explained to him by the President of the Elders . . .

In his eloquent and inspiring sermon, which was fully worthy of the event, [Rabbi] Dr Gaon said that the synagogue served as a reminder to the Jew of his duty to God and to humanity. It reflected the aspirations of the Jews as well as their fortunes. It was in this country, said the Haham [Rabbi], that Jews who had been persecuted in Spain and Portugal had found refuge . . . they were the fathers of the Anglo-Jewish community as it was known today.

The Haham recalled the interest taken by members of the Royal Family in the Congregation since the days of their first synagogue in Creechurch Lane, which Princess (later Queen) Anne had visited in 1685. They were grateful, he said, to the Duke of Edinburgh, who had revived that noble tradition. Dr Gaon also spoke of the liberal traditions of the City of London and expressed his pleasure at the presence of its representatives . . .

The Duke said that he had enjoyed the service, particularly the music, and he was interested to learn that the Sefardi Congregation had also a woman Elder . . . Mr F. Nabarro, Chairman of the Anniversary Committee, said that they invited the Duke because Princess Anne was yet too young to be able to repeat the visit to their congregation which her Royal namesake made over 250 years ago . . .

The synagogue gift shop

As American Jewry became *more established after World War I, a group of women formed what is now the Women's League of Conservative Judaism. Denied both a role in running their synagogues and professional careers, they undertook roles in Jewish education through publications and workshops. In particular they developed the concept of the synagogue gift shop, which had several effects: it gave an opportunity for the volunteers working in the shop to learn about Judaism, it promoted craftsmen and artists working in pre-State Palestine, and it fostered pride in Jewish traditions.*

This is an extract from The Jewish Home Beautiful, *a manual first published by the National Women's League of the United Synagogue of America in 1941. It encourages the homemaker to adopt the custom of having an elaborate festive meal on Purim, as well as promoting the purchase of Jewish-themed arts and crafts. The role of woman as homemaker was an essential part of American life in the 1940s and 1950s. Advertisements and stores stressed the idea that the lives of women could be fulfilled if they devoted themselves to making their home and their meals as attractive as possible. The editors of* The Jewish Home Beautiful, *Betty D. Greenberg and Althea O. Silverman, developed this viewpoint into an opportunity to spread Jewish learning.*

> The Table should be very gay and colorful; set for a Purim Seudah [meal], a dinner for eight people, service plates, silver, glassware, etc. The color scheme might be gold and red or blue—a gold cloth, red roses for the

centerpiece, red or blue candles and red or blue glass-ware, goblets and wine cups. A small doll richly dressed as Queen Esther may be perched on a tiny throne in the center of the flowers. If a glass horse is available, a figure dressed in purple as Mordecai should be sitting on the horse which is led by another figure dressed as the villainous Haman. This group is placed to one side of the centerpiece. On the other side is propped an illustrated Megillah [scroll of the Book of Esther] partly unrolled. If desired a huge platter containing a goose or other fowl of paper mache or clay may be placed on the table with a carving set nearby. At each setting is a gragor or noise-maker, a paper cap and mask, and a small dish of nuts . . . In a corner is a small open chest of coins for the poor.

A Friday Afternoon in Detroit, 1970:
The day the music died

Professor Sholom Kalib is the author of a monumental thesaurus, The Musical Tradition of the Eastern European Synagogue. *These are extracts from the introduction to Volume 1.*

Kalib grew up in Chicago and then became a cantor in Detroit. Here he describes an incident in his synagogue where he was due to lead the Friday evening service. This service is typically preceded by the short afternoon service (minhah), chanted by a competent layman.

The musical tradition of the eastern European synagogue represents one of the great sacred traditions of the world. During the period it flourished, from c.1675 to c. 1960, it rendered musical expression to the liturgy of the group which constituted the largest community within world Jewry . . .

With the gradual attrition of the older congregants from eastern Europe, succeeding American generations with little and often no Jewish education lacked the background and knowledge to fully participate, and in many cases to even follow a traditional Hebrew service . . . The artist-hazzan, the central figure within the musical tradition of the eastern European synagogue for over three centuries, has in essence ceased to exist in today's orthodox as well as liberal synagogues . . . Today's bleak status of synagogue music universally, which is at its lowest ebb in a number of essential aspects since the Middle Ages, makes the present work [the thesaurus] so compelling a necessity . . .

On Chicago's west side, through the decade of the 1940s, there was little evidence of the effect of acculturation in the synagogue and its traditional music. In the early 1950s, however, when Jewish people moved en masse to new neighborhoods, it became apparent that an ominous change was taking place . . . I began to ponder how seriously and quickly the obvious level of acculturation would encroach further . . .

It was not until the year 1970 that I witnessed the answers to those questions. The occasion was a Friday evening service in a synagogue in Detroit . . . when a layman ascended the pulpit to lead the minhah (afternoon) service. Though knowledgeable in the ritual and the Hebrew text, he had no apparent awareness of the existence of an appropriate nusah (traditional chant) . . . There was no evidence throughout the congregation that anyone else had. The thought instantly struck me: this is the inevitability I had begun to fear since the mid-1950s . . . Awareness by the community as a whole of the existence of nusah . . . had died. Then what understanding or appreciation could there be for hazzanut [cantorial art], which embellishes upon it? . . . The knowledgeable kahal [congregation] . . . had vanished into history.

Other cantors have similarly reflected on these historic changes. Here Cantors Samuel Rosenbaum and Saul Meisels, officers of the Cantors Assembly of New York, introduce a volume of synagogue congregational melodies (1974):

In days now gone by, the congregation participated in the best way, it davened, it prayed, listened, and appreciated the inspiration of the hazzan and allowed his music to inspire them to further prayer.

As the literacy of Jewish congregations decreased, a new means had to be found to interest and to involve congregants . . . Congregational singing is one such means.

Congregational singing is, however, more than a collection of tunes with which we hope to amuse the congregation. Congregational melodies, like the nusah of the hazzan, must be founded on tradition . . . A prayer service dare not become a mindless community sing . . .

Twenty-one years later, Cantor Rosenbaum reported to the Cantors Assembly on what his colleagues had told him in their appraisal of "the state of our faith . . . our unhappiness with our shrinking liturgy together with its appropriate chant, which go to make up the act we know as prayer."

We covered our major fears and misgivings . . . the shrinking service, the death of the choir and the concomitant burial or banishment to the hazzan's dead file of so many choral treasures. The almost total disregard of the age-old discipline of nusah which constitutes the heart and soul of our prayer traditions. The seeming inability of the congregation to understand that to sit and to listen, in an ambience of sanctity, is participation . . . That to mumble, or to articulate the Hebrew text clearly, is to participate . . .

The sound of silence: in 1997 Cantor Robert Kieval reported to the Cantors Assembly Convention:

Davening . . . is an alien function to most of our congregants today . . . I said to my hazzan sheni [deputy] this morning at davening [at the Convention], "This is something that we don't hear at the daily minyan any more, that hum of people davening, murmuray [murmuring]. All you hear is silence."

Eldridge Street Synagogue, Lower East Side, New York, 1971

IN 1971, NEW YORK University lecturer Gerard R. Wolfe was making a study of New York architecture when he stumbled on an apparently abandoned synagogue on Eldridge Street. After numerous enquiries he discovered that the basement of the building was used on Shabbat and holidays. He made contact with the shamash, Benjamin Markowitz, who let him into the basement on a November day in 1971. Here are extracts from Wolfe's account of that visit.

Mr Markowitz pointed to the pair of heavy wooden doors leading upstairs to the main sanctuary, but they were nailed shut with thick planks. I was able to persuade him to help me pry the planks off, which he did somewhat hesitantly, and we were then able to force the badly warped doors open and pass through to the staircase landing inside. Mr Markowitz chose to remain behind and go no further. I then proceeded gingerly, in almost total darkness, up the shaky wooden staircase until I saw light streaming in through the broken glass panels of the vestibule doors above.

As my eyes grew accustomed to the half-light in the foyer, I saw that there were yellowed newspapers strewn about on the floor, dated 1933 . . . Eerie sounds were made by scores of cooing pigeons as they fluttered and huddled in the overhead rafters.

Moving carefully, I tried to open the doors to the sanctuary, only to discover that they were solidly warped shut. I shoved hard on the doors with all my strength.

For a few moments they resisted my efforts. Finally the doors gave way as they slowly creaked open. I will never forget the exhilaration and awe I experienced as I took my first hesitant steps into that darkened sanctuary. As if transported to another, more ancient spiritual world, I was stunned into silence by an unexpected and dramatic vision of grandeur and majesty.

Immediately, the sight of an enormous and ornate brass chandelier dazzled me—its dozens of Victorian etched glass shades still intact—suspended from the immense seventy-foot-high barrel-vaulted ceiling. I could easily imagine how in the distant past, the gas-lit fixtures must have filled the enormous sanctuary with an aura of soft amber-coloured light . . . The striking stained glass windows that lined the sanctuary walls and the upstairs gallery commanded my attention . . . Torn strips of trompe l'oeil murals, deeply stained decorative wall stenciling, and brass wall lamps topped by crown-like features all hung askew. Everything was covered with dust and cobwebs—presenting an unbelievable picture of faded glory and awesome magnificence . . . The Ark was made of Italian walnut and contained twenty-four aging Torahs tightly wrapped in their original red velvet cases . . .

Stunned by the immensity and overwhelming beauty and fragility of the room, I literally staggered back down the rickety staircase to share excitedly with Mr Markowitz what I had just seen . . .

Wolfe wrote about his discovery in the New York Times *and immediately the synagogue received offers of financial support. The restored synagogue was reopened in 2007 at a cost of $20 million. Officially named Khal Adath Jeshurun - Anshe Lubz, when opened in 1887 it was New York City's first purpose-built synagogue by and for immigrant eastern European Jews.*

Odessa, U.S.S.R., 1981

From "In Search of the Lost Jews of Russia"
by George Feifer, The Sunday Times Magazine

Odessa's synagogue is not, as one of the most authorita-
tive recent accounts of Russian life identifies it, a former
fur factory. It might as well be. In a muddy district of
warehouses and rotting communal flats, I picked my
way through a tough crowd jostling for position at a stall
selling stunted apples, then stepped over two drunks em-
bracing in the grime at the bottom of a beer booth.

Nothing distinguished the exterior of the building
from the dingy ones flanking it. There were no signs of
life—no-one answered my knock. At last a flap opened
a crack to allow a pair of frightened, hostile eyes to ex-
amine me. "Who are you? What do you want here?" was
another way of saying, "Go away, let us at least die in
peace" . . .

More than a hundred synagogues had functioned in
Odessa. The pearl of them, a once glorious temple [the
Brodsky Synagogue] on Pushkin Street in the most elegant district, is now a repository for records of the city's
Communist Party organization. Angry guards stopped
me when I tried to peek inside. All the others have also
been closed, converted to other uses, or destroyed . . .

A ninety-year-old worshiper assured me that "no
young people ever come", apart from two or three annual
holidays. The congregation has no rabbi. The two dozen
pensioners who celebrate the Sabbath every week sup-
pose the synagogue will close when they die . . .

When I tried to discuss this—alone, of course—with a Jewish official in publishing, he dismissed the subject with a wave. The synagogue's difficulties concerned him least of all. "Nobody's really interested in the twilight of a few old geezers. Maybe it's tragic, but it's not high on the list of our tragedies at the moment."

The Soviet Union collapsed in 1991, seventy years after its creation. There are now several functioning synagogues in Odessa, including the historic Brodsky Synagogue. There are schools and kosher restaurants, and a Jewish Museum which has a large sign over the entrance in Hebrew and Russian: "Modern Israel was born here."

Looking for a minyan at the Bayreuth Festival, 1983

By Harold Rosenthal

Although this was regarded as British year at Bayreuth, with the Solti-Peter Hall new production of "The Ring" in which several British artists sang, it was also Jewish year.

In addition to Solti, who of course conducted the new production, there was Daniel Barenboim in the pit for "Tristan und Isolde" and James Levine for "Parsifal". Cosima Wagner, I am sure, must have turned in her grave!

I have in my possession a pre-Hitler street map of Bayreuth which shows the existence of a synagogue just behind the old Margrave's Opera House.

Few know of the existence of the synagogue, but a South African critic and musician, Leonard Schach, and Solti knew about it. Sir Georg decided that, with three Jewish conductors in Bayreuth, the synagogue should be unlocked and a Friday night service held during the first week of the Festival.

The keys of the synagogue, which were held by Bayreuth's police chief (who is half-Jewish), were produced for Solti. My colleague Max Loppert, music critic of the "Financial Times," was asked by Solti if he would help make up a minyan and he readily agreed.

Unfortunately, there was a crisis at the Festival Opera House, the East German Siegfried having left after the dress rehearsal, and Solti had to abandon the plan. However, as he will be returning to Bayreuth next year (and no doubt Levine as well, if not Barenboim), one hopes that the synagogue will be used for the purpose for which it was built . . .

Pope's historic visit

From Tullia Zevi, Rome, April 18, 1986

Sunday's historic visit to the main synagogue in Rome by Pope John Paul II, the first in history by a Pope to a Jewish house of worship, has been widely acclaimed by religious and lay circles of both faiths in the Italian capital . . . When the Pope gave his address, he quoted from the document on the Jews issued by the second Vatican Ecumenical Council in 1965, which deplored "the hatred, persecutions and displays of anti-semitism directed against the Jews at any time and by anyone".

"I wish my grandmother could have seen this. She was born and bred in the Rome Ghetto," said an elderly communal leader, with tears in his eyes . . . There was a widespread feeling among Rome's Jews that, somehow, the unprecedented occasion had drawn a line under centuries of segregation and humiliation, leading to Christian-Jewish dialog and co-operation . . .

In his address, [Chief] Rabbi Toaff advocated dialogue and common efforts among believers of different faiths to improve the lot of humanity. He also urged the Pope to accord recognition to Israel . . . "The return of the Jewish people to its land must be recognized . . . because it leads, according to the teachings of the Prophets, to the time of universal brotherhood towards which we all strive . . ."

The Pope failed to respond . . . Qualified sources, including Rabbi Toaff, believe, however, that there may be a change in the not too distant future . . .

In his synagogue address, the Pope acknowledged that "we have a relationship with Judaism which we do not have with any other religion. You are our dearly beloved brothers and, in a certain way, it could be said that you are our elder brothers . . ."

"Stop throwing us crumbs"

Haaretz, *Oct 30, 2017*

A senior representative of Israel's government tried to reassure world Jewish leaders on Monday that Prime Minister Benjamin Netanyahu remains committed to the recently suspended Western Wall agreement . . . "The few crumbs the government has said it will throw our way it will continue to throw our way," said Rabbi Rick Jacobs, president of the Union for Reform Judaism . . . "These crumbs are unacceptable" . . .

In January 2016, the government approved an agreement to provide the Reform and Conservative movements with an upgraded, egalitarian prayer plaza at the southern side of the Western Wall. Under that arrangement, the plaza would be as accessible as the existing area for gender-segregated worship on the northern side . . . [Deputy minister] Hanegbi told the delegation of Jewish leaders that the government intends to invest millions of dollars in upgrading the makeshift plaza currently used for mixed-gender services, in the area known as Robinson's Arch. He said the government would also take into consideration the demand that the egalitarian space be fully visible and accessible to visitors to the Western Wall. It is currently hidden behind a tall fence and accessible only by stairs; there are no signs at the entrance to the Western Wall indicating its location.

But Hanegbi rejected out of hand the demand . . . that the permanent plaza for egalitarian worship will share an entrance with the gender-segregated area, as had initially been agreed on by the government . . .

Along with Women of the Wall, the feminist prayer group, the Reform and Conservative movements petitioned the Supreme Court a year ago, demanding that the government either fulfill the so-called original "Wall deal" or re-divide the gender-segregated prayer space to make room for non-orthodox worshipers. The petition was submitted before the government officially voted to suspend the agreement . . .

The meeting at the Wall, which was organized by Jewish Agency Chairman Nathan Sharansky, was held in the makeshift egalitarian prayer space. After Hanegbi departed, Sharansky said he was not deeply disappointed by the outcome because he hadn't come with high hopes.

At the Western Wall

The Jerusalem Post, *July 13, 2018*

Activists from the Women of the Wall feminist organization were violently attacked during the group's monthly prayer service at the Western Wall Friday morning, members of the group told *The Jerusalem Post.*

A mob of haredi [ultra-orthodox] men threw rocks at activists, a Jewish prayerbook bearing the Women of the Wall insignia was burned, and a young American intern for the organization had to seek medical treatment for wounds to the head and neck, activists said.

The group of some two hundred activists, dressed in the ritual prayer shawls and yarmulkas that traditional Judaism prescribes only for men, had gathered at the Western Wall to mark the beginning of the Hebrew month of Av. During the service, ultra-orthodox women in the same gender-segregated section of the Western Wall plaza harassed the Women of the Wall activists, the organization said in a statement released Friday . . .

When the group left the Western Wall plaza they encountered an angry group of haredi men . . . Shira Boyar, an intern with the organization from Sharon, Massachusetts and an incoming senior at Connecticut College, was physically assaulted . . . Boyar and four friends fled the scene, but they were pursued by the mob. "My boyfriend tried to call the police," she said. "They asked, 'Who's chasing you?' When he said, 'Haredim,' they replied, 'Oh, it's not Arabs? Okay, okay, we'll send someone when we can.'" The police, she said, never arrived.

November 3, 2018: #ShowUpForShabbat

ON THE MORNING OF *Saturday October 27, 2018, a gunman en-*
tered the Tree of Life Synagogue, Pittsburgh, yelled: "All Jews must
die," and opened fire, killing eleven people—the deadliest attack
on Jews in American history. (One month earlier, members of the
synagogue had been trained to deal with just such an "Intentional
Mass Casualty Event". The training included the use of cell phones,
even though this is normally prohibited on Shabbat—it is a Jewish
principle that pikuah nefesh, *saving life, overrides all other laws.)*
The gunman was eventually shot and wounded by police and taken
into custody. It later emerged that the gunman used far-right web-
sites and was partly motivated by the Jewish community's actions
in supporting immigrants. Later that week President Donald Trump
visited Pittsburgh, and was met by a demonstration against white
nationalism. The mayor did not meet him, but Rabbi Hazzan Jeff
Myers said: "The president of the United States is always welcome."

Synagogues around the world publicized their services the
following Shabbat under the Twitter hashtag #ShowUpForShab-
bat, and large numbers of people who would otherwise not go to
synagogue were moved to attend. The events and their impact were
widely covered in newspapers:

> London Mayor Sadiq Khan was among those who at-
> tended synagogue on Saturday as part of the "Show up
> for Shabbat" initiative after the Pittsburgh shooting . . .
> Rabbi Neil Janes implored people at West London Syna-
> gogue to "focus on amplifying small and yet simple acts
> so that the voices of hope are louder than those of hate

. . . I cannot tell you how truly sustaining and significant the small act of sitting in pews with us all across the world has become."

The mayor called the service "deeply moving", adding: "London stands shoulder-to-shoulder with the Jewish community here and around the world. Last week Jews were gunned down in pews like these, today in defiance we sit together with the human family to strive to increase the goodness in the world, to bring light to darkness . . ."

As my husband and I approached Holy Blossom Temple in Toronto, we saw buses parked outside. They had carried Muslims and Christians who were standing shoulder-to-shoulder, forming a ring of peace around our building . . . Once the service began, I looked around to see a sanctuary filled from the first to the very last row with Jews, all of whom wanted to be together. Scattered among our members were many non-Jews, Muslims, Christians and some government leaders—tangible evidence of the outpouring of unity, solidarity and compassion for their Jewish brethren . . .

Amanda Golden, a producer for CNN . . . shared on Twitter the text messages that her mother, a first-generation American and the daughter of Holocaust survivors sent to her . . . "Important not to be alone. That is why I go to Temple. Not to feel alone with these feelings."

In the days leading up to the shooting, I was on a press trip on a cruise ship. I had joined the last three days of a two-week tour, and by the time I got there the passengers were deeply into the rhythm of their holiday. Routines had long since been established and friendships formed. So when, on the Friday night, my husband and I entered the room that had been set up in preparation for a Shabbat service, the group of Jewish guests there greeted us with warmth and amazement. Who were we? Why hadn't they met us yet? How come we were only on board for three days? Was that even allowed? A press trip? For which paper? And so on.

Then the service began, carried out jointly by all present. At first, it was a halting affair. People were not quite sure which bits to read or which tune anyone else was going to know. And yet, it all came together, the Shema, the Amidah, the Kaddish flowing off the tongues of this geographically disparate group and giving it instant unity. For the rest of the time on the ship, whenever someone who had been at the service spotted us, they hailed us like old friends.

It was really very simple—we felt connected because we were all Jewish, and so it is with the community in Pittsburgh. An attack on a Jewish community anywhere feels like an attack on our own.

Rabbis avoid calling Tree of Life a synagogue

By Anshel Pfeffer in Jerusalem,
Jewish Chronicle, *2 November, 2018*

Israel's chief rabbis drew a rare rebuke from Prime Minister Benjamin Netanyahu after they would not describe the site of the Pittsburgh shooting as a synagogue. Ashkenazi Chief Rabbi David Lau and his Sephardi colleague Rabbi Yitzhak Yosef put out statements condemning the murders and expressing their solidarity with American Jews, but both refused to call the Tree of Life a synagogue. In an interview with the *Makor Rishon* website, Rabbi Lau repeatedly refused to be drawn on the matter, describing it only as "a place which was considered by the murderer to have a conspicuous Jewish identity. A place with Torah scrolls, Jews with tallitot and siddurim. There are people there who came to seek the closeness of God." Despite the interviewer's persistent questioning, he would not use the word "synagogue". In a similar vein, Israel's Haredi newspapers referred to it as "a Jewish center".

The Israeli rabbis' stance . . . highlighted a much deeper tension between the two largest Jewish communities in the world: in Israel, where progressive Jews are a small minority; and the United States, where they are a majority . . .

The publicity surrounding Rabbi Lau's interview led to the Prime Minister's intervention—a rare move, because Mr Netanyahu is usually careful not to say anything that could anger his strictly orthodox political allies. In a short statement that did not mention the Chief Rabbi, Mr Netanyahu said: "Jews were killed in a synagogue. They were killed because they are Jews. The location was chosen because it is a synagogue . . ."

The Synagogue in the Twenty-First Century
Worship in the Post-Shul Era

SHUL GOING DOES NOT *seem well suited to the twenty-first century. Reform rabbis describe services as "sterile" or "boring". Orthodox rabbis are faced with congregations that no longer passively attend synagogue but instead demand programs offering them a reason to attend. Many in the congregation simply do not know what the service is about.*

Faced with the collapse of traditional congregations, synagogue officials are searching for alternative forms of worship.

The following pages are samples of innovations for the twenty-first century.

High Holy Days at the Song Shul, Toronto

There is no other service like this anywhere . . .
Look who's at The Song Shul for Yamim Noraim!
Will you be there, too?

STELLAR SPEAKERS
The Honourable Linda Frum, Member of the Senate of Canada
Paul Godfrey, President and CEO of Postmedia Network
Shai Deluca-Tamasi, Television Personality, Former IDF Member
Dr Brian Goldman, Author of *The Power of Kindness*

SPECIAL MUSICAL GUEST
Mark Masri, Grammy and Juno-Award Nominee
PLUS
Lauren Tatner, leading Spiritual Meditation and Relaxation

LUXURIOUS SEATING in the magnificent George Weston Recital Hall at the Toronto Centre for the Arts
COMPELLING DISCUSSION GROUPS for teens, university students and young adults
FABULOUS CHILDREN'S PROGRAMS AND ACTIVITIES
BABYSITTING AVAILABLE
COMPLIMENTARY ROSH HASHANAH COFFEE LOUNGE
AND MUCH MORE!

THE SONG SHUL'S DREAM TEAM

World renowned Cantor SIMON SPIRO accompanied by the Toronto Festival Singers . . .

ALIZA SPIRO, dynamically guiding us through the services

Earth-based Jewish experiences

Shoresh Jewish Environmental Program,
Bela Farm, Hillsburgh, Ontario

SHORESH IS ONE OF *several Jewish agricultural initiatives that have sprung up around the world in recent years. It runs Jewish educational programs and provides farm products for the Jewish community, motivated by the very ethics that are stressed in Jewish literature. It specifically seeks to attract those who do not attend a synagogue. There is a focus on those Jewish holidays that were originally agricultural, such as Tu B'Shvat.*

CONTEXT

Shoresh's programs and activities respond to three key challenges facing our community:

Environmental crisis: The effects of environmental degradation are being felt in devastating ways . . . Honey bee populations being decimated by agricultural pesticides; an island of plastics the size of Texas floating in the Pacific Ocean; and severe and unpredictable weather events due to global climate change . . .

Poverty and hunger: . . . Within our own community, over 24,000 Toronto Jews are living below the poverty line . . . the majority of them lacking access to fresh, local, organic, healthy food.

Jewish disengagement: . . . Individuals from across the Jewish spectrums, young adults in particular, are struggling to find engaging and meaningful experiences that strengthen their Jewish identity and facilitate sustainable action and community building.

VALUES AND OUTCOMES

As a Jewish charity, we respond to these complex imbalances in our world and our community through educational programs and actions grounded in Jewish ethics. The following are the core values that guide our programs . . . as well as the outcomes we aspire to achieve through our work of *Tikkun Olam,* repairing the world.

Mah rabu ! How Great! Foster a sense of awe and wonder at the natural world in order to inspire responsible stewardship of Earth and its resources.

L'ovdah ul'shomrah. To work and protect. Support sustainable environmental practices . . .

Dayenu. Enough. Promote gratitude for existing resources and avoid wasteful choices . . .

Tzedek, tzedek tirdof. Justice, justice you shall pursue. Respond to hunger in our community . . .

Kehillah. Community. Build a more cohesive, pluralistic, and interconnected Jewish community, united by a shared relationship with the natural world.

Zehut. Identity. Deepen personal Jewish identity through earth-based Jewish experiences, reconnecting community members with their Jewish roots.

Contemporary issues and uncertainties in a future Mayan ruin

THE SYNAGOGUE IN REICHSHOFFEN, French Alsace, was last used in 1967. A Jewish community had lived on that site for five hundred years, surviving the Thirty Years War and the Holocaust.

In 2018, the Israeli-Italian artist Yoav Rossano, living in nearby Strasbourg, created an art installation in the abandoned synagogue to draw attention to the site, which many local inhabitants were unaware of.

"The first step to overcome this ignorance is to promote awareness of the region's past," says Rossano. For the last two years he has been working with Ben Jack Nash, a British artist also based in Strasbourg. Nash says he was eerily drawn to the synagogue's quiet presence from his first visit. After researching the site and interviewing the local community, he developed a project, *Les Résidus du Vide (Remains of the Void)*, which aims to breathe new life into the building.

He has created a large-scale art installation that uses sculpture, light and movement to transform the interior of the building into "a place for reflection, question, and connection". In particular, the art interacts with the site's striking stained glass windows, stone carvings, and other original features. "The art was created to relate to the synagogue's features and personality. It reverses the traditional role of art exhibitions by making the art the backdrop for the exhibition space. It is important that the work is not seen as a mausoleum for the past, rather that it connects with contemporary issues and uncertainties.

"The communities who cared for Reichshoffen and similar sites are long gone. Current communities don't have that connection so they go unloved . . . The fate of these sites does not lie in the hands of some handout from the EU or a trust foundation. It has to come from the living communities. These future Mayan ruins are as much part of local history and identity as castles and monasteries . . ."

Challenging assumptions

Temple Sinai Congregation of Toronto held a unique Slichot service on September 5 that Rabbi Michael Dolgin, the Reform synagogue's senior rabbi, said can be categorized as "neither show nor shul."

As part of a larger effort to challenge people's assumptions about prayer, Temple Sinai created an innovative Slichot [penitential prayers before Rosh Hashanah] by fusing traditional Jewish writings with Jewish theatrical texts and traditional synagogue music with music one would find in a Jewish theater production . . .

The service was held at the Toronto Centre for the Arts and drew a crowd of over seven hundred people.

The service featured two cantors, two rabbis, four actors, three singers, and a ten-piece orchestra . . .

In addition to traditional liturgy . . . the program included a dramatic telling of the story of Israeli astronaut Ilan Ramon, a rendition of Bette Midler's song *From A Distance*, a scene from Rich Orloff's play *Can This Marriage Be Saved* . . . and an improvised skit . . .

Rabbi Dolgin explained that the purpose of the night was to give congregants or any interested members of the Jewish community a "chance to prepare for the holidays in a way we believe would be more accessible to people who wouldn't attend shul with regularity . . . a new kind of Jewish communal prayer . . . this mixture of traditional liturgy, teaching and cultural and musical pieces . . . A lot of people are hungry for [different kinds of] spiritual experiences . . . We hope the collaboration with the theater company can help provide that."

Let's be honest

It's quarter to eleven on a Saturday morning at Hampstead Garden Suburb United Synagogue [in north-west London] . . . The reader of the haftarah is getting ready to chant the weekly portion of the Prophets. Before he starts, a number of people will have quietly slipped out of the main synagogue . . . They head off to the synagogue library where for the next forty-five minutes they will take part in "Coffee and Conversation". It may not sound particularly revolutionary, but for a mainstream orthodox congregation in London to hold a break-out session mid-service is a departure . . . "The whole concept [says founder Martin Kaye] was to appeal to those who don't come to shul, and those who do but wish they hadn't" . . . Topics have ranged from Jewish pirates of the Caribbean to [Jewish holidays] . . . After the session people can stay around talking to the speaker or go into the main service . . .

The United Synagogue found that three out of every five members said services were important in their choice of synagogue but fewer than two out of five found them engaging . . . The Coffee and Conversation sessions are particularly popular with women . . . "It's difficult to sit in the women's gallery [said one woman], you feel a bit detached. As I get older, I find it harder and harder" . . .

"Let's be honest" says Rabbi Dov Kaplan, "so many are disengaged from Shabbat morning services because they are long and people don't get the meaning" . . . Officially the synagogue can't encourage people to skip parts of the service, so the start of the education session is not announced on Saturday morning . . .

DO SHUL DIFFERENTLY

In an effort to encourage innovation among its congregations, the [London] United Synagogue is offering matching funding to creative projects . . . The idea is to "do shul differently" . . . The latest tranche of projects include Woodside Park Synagogue's Generation to Generation research study, the idea of congregant and women's historian Michelle Rosenberg. It will enable congregants to work with a professional genealogist to trace important women in their own families—and also Jewish women who have made an impact on history. Mrs Rosenberg says her daughter's bat mitzvah [coming of age] brought home to her that "as women, we couldn't follow the service well and didn't feel as if we were being represented, or had opportunities to feel a part of the community" . . . She hopes that women involved in the project will deliver brief talks about their discoveries . . . "I think this will help women to feel part of the service" . . .

ALTERNATIVE MINYANIM

At Kol Nidre this year, a visitor would have been able to walk into Hendon United Synagogue in north-west London and comfortably find a seat. Twenty years ago, for one of the twenty-five biggest congregations in the country not to have been full would have been inconceivable. While the main service could still boast the pomp of hazzan and choir, elsewhere in the building two alternative minyanim catered for a younger age group . . .

The alternative minyan has become a standard feature of twenty-first-century worship. Big "multiplex" synagogues can offer three, even four minyanim on a Saturday, not to mention youth and children's services . . .

"Many years ago the view was that everyone had to be in one service," said US president Stephen Pack . . . The alternative minyan is typically more informal than the "high synagogue" style of old Anglo-Jewry . . . New tunes from Israel or the USA prevail . . . They are more participatory, led by members rather than by hazzan or rabbi. "People want to get more involved and be more hands-on" . . .

Judith Williams, who heads the Reform Jeneration [young adult] department, believes [independent] groups . . . should not be seen as competition for synagogues but as an investment for the future. "Synagogue affiliation may be down," she said, "but the need to belong has not changed . . ."

A CROWD-SOURCING SYNAGOGUE

The City Shul, affiliated with the Reform Movement, was founded in downtown Toronto in 2012, under the leadership of Rabbi Elyse Goldstein.

The synagogue is taking the approach of building its policies and traditions through its congregation. "Decisions and policies are now being invented, are now being imagined together with the congregation," Rabbi Goldstein said. "It's very much a crowd-sourcing synagogue" . . . After the High Holiday services, the synagogue sent a survey to people who attended to find out which parts of the services they found meaningful and which parts they would like to change for next time . . .

Some members are orthodox Jews, others are interfaith couples, spiritual searchers and even people with no Jewish background . . . The shul's programing attracts a wide range of people. For example, each month there will be two Friday night services. One is for families with children, with a story and a potluck dinner. The other is for adults and includes a one-hour musical meditation to welcome in Shabbat. Rabbi Goldstein described the shul's services as very traditional . . .

TRANSCENDING POSTCODES

Mishkan *was founded in London in 2016 by Rabbi Naftali and Dina Brawer. The following extracts are taken from advertisements and interviews which appeared in the London* Jewish Chronicle *in 2016 and 2017. "Mishkan" is the Hebrew for "Tabernacle", also referred to as "the tent of meeting", the portable Sanctuary which the Israelites carried with them in the desert.*

Mishkan is a Jewish community that transcends post-codes and fixed spaces. We understand community in a twenty-first-century context, as individuals bound by shared spaces. We strive to create meaningful religious experiences using public spaces such as cafes, pubs, and art galleries as well as private homes. In these spaces we study, discuss and pray, connect with each other, engage in tzedakah [charity] and tikkun olam . . .

"We are looking to augment what traditional communities offer by curating content-rich Jewish experiences in a more flexible framework," Dina Brawer explained.

The High Holiday Playlist:

Immersive Prayer for Personal Transformation

Rosh Hashanah: Sync and Charge

Yom Kippur: Reinventing Yourself

Construct a meaningful service from a selection of modular units, blending traditional prayer with storytelling, niggunim (soulful hasidic melodies), poetry and visual art

Join us for the entire day or choose which units you wish to attend

All services take place at The Big Tent of Meeting in Borehamwood

Walking to Caesarea

O God,
May there never cease to be
The sand and the sea,
The water's murmurs,
The sky's brilliance,
Man's prayer.

From the Hebrew of Hannah Szenes

Glossary

I HAVE GIVEN ALTERNATIVE spellings as they occur in different sources. Plural forms have -*im* or -*ot* at the end of the word.

Amidah: Prayer recited standing and in silence

Ark: Closet in which the scrolls of the Torah are housed

Ashkenazi: (As opposed to Sefardi), originating from northern Europe

Baal tefilah: Prayer leader

Bar mitzvah: Coming of age for a boy at 13

Bet midrash (beth midrash, beth medresh): Schoolhouse which is also used as a synagogue

Bimah (Bima): Platform for public reading of the Torah

Cholent: Meat stew served on the Sabbath

Daven: Pray

Elul: The month preceding Rosh Hashanah

Haftarah: Scriptural Lesson from the Prophets

Halakhah: Jewish law

Haredi (Charedi): "Ultra orthodox"

Hasidim: Ultra-orthodox sects, originating in eastern Europe in the late eighteenth century, whose worship is closely attached to a charismatic rabbi and which emphasises singing

Hazzan: Cantor, prayer leader selected for his knowledge and vocal ability

High Holydays/Holidays: Yamim Noraim, the New Year holidays from Rosh Hashanah through Yom Kippur in the fall

Hoshana Rabbah: The seventh day of Sukkot, in some respects an echo of Yom Kippur

Kabbalah: Jewish mysticism, sometimes bordering on magic

Kaddish: Prayer said at every service; also recited by mourners

Kiddush: Ritual drinking of wine on Sabbath and holidays, accompanied by snacks

Kiddush Hashem: "Sanctification of God's name", an honorable deed, often meaning martyrdom

Kippah: Skullcap

Kohen (pl. kohanim): A member of the hereditary priesthood; in modern times a kohen has the authority to bless the community, and has certain minor privileges

Kol Nidrei (Nidre): The solemn opening prayer on Yom Kippur evening

Maariv: Evening prayers

Midrash: Literature created by the Rabbis in Talmudic times

Minhah (minchah): Afternoon prayers

Minyan: Quorum of ten men needed for a service

Mishnah: Code of Jewish law, edited in the second century

Mitzvah: "Commandment", any Jewish law; a "good deed"

Musaf: Additional service on Sabbath and holidays

Ne'ilah: The solemn service which concludes Yom Kippur

Nusah: Musical mode used in liturgy, appropriate to the occasion

Piyyut (piyut): Elaborate liturgical poem

Purim: Carnival-like holiday in late winter celebrating the story of Esther

Rosh Hashanah: The solemn New Year festival in the fall

Rosh Hodesh: New Moon, a minor holiday with additional prayers

Sefardi (Sephardi): (As opposed to Ashkenazi), originating from Spain/North Africa

Shema: Recitation of Deut 6:4–9, the core profession of faith

Siddur: Prayerbook

Shabbat: Sabbath, Saturday

Shamash: Beadle, sexton, synagogue assistant

Shtetl: Small town

Simhat Torah: The last day of Sukkot, a day of merriment

Slichot (selihot): Penitential prayers recited before Rosh Hashanah

Sukkot: Thanksgiving holiday in the fall

Tallit (Tallis): Prayer shawl worn by men

Talmud: Compendium of opinions on Jewish law, edited around the end of the fifth century. There are two versions, one compiled in Jerusalem and one in Babylon. In this book all references are to the Babylonian Talmud

Talmud Torah: School

Tefillin: A pair of leather boxes containing scriptural verses, worn on the arm and head during morning prayers

Tikkun olam: "Repairing the world", usually taken to mean programs of social justice or environmental awareness

Torah: The Five Books of Moses; in the broad sense, the entire body of Jewish teaching

Tu B'Shvat: Minor holiday in late winter, originally relating to agriculture

Yamim Noraim: "Days of Awe", High Holydays/Holidays at New Year

Yarmulka: Skullcap

Yeshivah: Talmudical college

Yizkor: Memorial prayer for the dead

Yom Kippur: Day of Atonement, a day of fasting and repentance

Yortsayt (Yahrzeit): The anniversary of a death, marked by special prayers

Sources

Jeremiah: Jer 29:4–7.

Ezekiel: Ezek 11:16–17.

Daniel: Dan 6:11–12, 17, 19–22.

Ezra: Neh 7:73, 8:1–3, 7–10, 12.

Egypt: See Reinach, "Sur la Date," 161–4.

Second Temple: See b. Sotah 40b–41a.

Men and women: See b. Sukkah 51b.

First-Century Jerusalem: This stone is reproduced in many publications and websites. The stone is on display at the Israel Museum, Jerusalem.

Ruins of Jerusalem: See b. Berakhot 3a.

Rome: Ovid, *Ars Amatoria* 1:75–6, 415–6.

Rabbi Eliezer: See b. Berakhot 34a.

Alexandria: See b. Sukkah 51b.

Jacob of Paris: See Adler, *Jewish Travellers,* 122–3.

Ramban: See Kobler, *Letters,* vol. 1, 226.

Meshullam of Volterra: See Adler, 161–2.

Ovadiah of Bertinoro: See Adler, 210–12, 222, 236, 243.

Akbar: See Hansen, *The Peacock Throne,* 399.

Tissard: See Tissard, Diii recto-verso. I am grateful to Prof. Anthony T. Grafton of Princeton for making this text available to me, and to Will Theiss for the translation from Latin.

Altneuschul: These Regulations are posted on the wall of the synagogue.

Leone: See Kobler, vol. 2, 416–8.

Jo. Greenhalgh: See Ellis, *Letters*, 3–21. On conversos, see Nadler, *Manasseh Ben Israel*.

Pepys: See Latham and Matthews, 334–6 (entry for October 14, 1663).

Burney: See Burney, 299–302.

Charleston: See Marcus, *American Jewry: Documents*, 183.

Plymouth: This prayer is inscribed on the wall of the synagogue.

Washington: His letter is reproduced in: Malcolm H. Stern. "Washington, George." In *Encyclopedia Judaica* 16: 359–61. The letter from the Privy Council is quoted in Roth, *History of the Jews in England*, 171.

Regency London: Zangwill, *The King of Schnorrers*, 1–3.

Sulzer/Trollope: See Trollope, *Vienna and the Austrians*, 373–4 (Letter XXXI, Vienna 30 October, 1836). The French quote is from Racine, *Esther* 1, 4.

Sulzer/Liszt: See Liszt, "Les Israélites," in *Des Bohémiens*, 73–6. Some of this is published in English in Morgenstern, *Composers on Music*, 163–4.

Sulzer/Hanslick: See Hanslick, *Aus Dem Concertsaal*, 400–402 (originally published in *Die Neue Freie Presse*, March 13, 1866). Some of this passage is quoted in English in Werner, *A Voice Still Heard*, 216–7.

New West End choir: From a leaflet c. 1889, New West End Synagogue archives.

Sydney: See Apple, *The Great Synagogue*, 12. The newspaper reports are from the *Sydney Morning Herald* and *The Town and Country Journal*.

Rev. Singer: Quoted in Vivian Lipman, "From ghetto to suburb," *Jewish Chronicle*, September 21, 1984.

Chevras: See Beatrice Potter, "The Jewish Community," in Booth, *Life and Labour*, 169–72.

Zogerin of Berdichev: See *The Zogerin: Interview with Efim Skobilitskii*, video produced by Indiana University: AHEYM: Yiddish Archives~aheym/profile.php?id=57.

Zogerin/Brokhes: See Rokhl Brokhes, trans. Shirley Kumove, "The Zogerin," in Forman, *Found Treasures*, 85–90.

Rio de Janeiro: See Vincent, *Bodies and Souls*, 205–6. The quote about "vile traffic" is from "The Jewish Colonies in the Argentine," *Jewish Chronicle*, November 4, 1892.

Glasgow: "Glasgow South Side Synagogue," *Jewish Chronicle*, September 13, 1901.

Kiever shul: Notice displayed in the synagogue.

Moscow: See Rosse, "The 'Choral Shool'", 12–14.

Golem: Meyrink, *The Golem*, 106-7, 110.

Passover eve in the shtetl: See Sholem Aleichem, "A Page From the Song of Songs," trans. Julius and Frances Butwin, in Howe, *Treasury*, 424–6.

Forverts: See Metzker, *Bintel Brief*, 97–98.

Yossele: See Rosenblatt, *Yossele Rosenblatt*, 14–15, 29–30, 95.

Franz Rosenzweig: See Glatzer, *Franz Rosenzweig*, 75–77

Cairo: See Roden, *Jewish Food*, 8.

Cambridge: See Cyril Domb, "Jewish Life at Cambridge in the 1930s and 1940s," in Frankel, 75–76. The quote from Raphael Loewe is from p. 22 of the same volume. CUJS as folklore: See Raphael Loewe, "The Evolution of Jewish Student Feeding

Arrangements in Oxford and Cambridge," *Studies in The Cultural Life of the Jews of England*, ed. D. Noy and I. Ben-Ami, Folklore Research Center Studies v, Jerusalem, 1975, 165f.

Schoenberg: See Stein, *Arnold Schoenberg: Letters*, 212–3. On the interview with Hazzan Putterman, see: Sam Pessaroff, "Commissioning Contemporary Composers", 7, 11–12. On Vinaver and *De Profundis*, see Vinaver, *Anthology*, 201-3. The phrase "smell of the synagogue" is from Rosenfeld, *Musical Portraits*, 241.

Stop the talking: Leaflet issued by stopthetalking@gmail.com. "Woe to those who talk during prayer" is from *Mishnah Brurah* 124:27

Tsemakh Atlas: Grade, *The Yeshiva*, vol. I, 257.

Valkenik: Grade, *The Yeshiva*, vol. II, *Masters and Disciples*, 70–72.

Western Wall, 1928: See *The Western or Wailing Wall in Jerusalem: Memorandum by the Secretary of State for the Colonies* (London: H.M.S.O., Cmd. 3229, 1928), 2-4.

Western Wall 1930 Commission: See *Report of the Commission . . . in connection with the Western or Wailing Wall at Jerusalem, December 1930* (London: H.M.S.O., 58-9096, 1931), 3, 7, 17, 60–61.

Mannheim: Transcribed from video: *Samuel Adler (2006): Life in Mannheim, Germany.* Robert H. Jackson Center, Jamestown, N.Y. www.youtube.com/watch?v=x5hnR13Cl8g.

Germany last minyan: Emil Lowenstein, "The school minyan that saved the day," *Jewish Chronicle*, November 4, 1988.

Bar mitzvah in Czestochowa: See Gutter, *Memories in Focus*, 2, 76–77, 80–81.

Vilna: Grade, *My Mother's Sabbath Days*, 386-8.

Great Synagogue: Frank Rose, "The glory of the Great," *Jewish Chronicle*, May 8, 1981.

Prince Philip: "Prince Philip at Bevis Marks," *Jewish Chronicle*, December 21, 1951.

Gift shop: See Betty D. Greenberg, *The Jewish Home Beautiful*, 71. See also Weiss, "A League of Their Own".

Detroit: Kalib, *The Musical Tradition*, foreword; Samuel Rosenbaum and Saul Meisels, foreword to Nathanson, *Zamru Lo* vol. 3; Samuel Rosenbaum, "Annual Report," 37–8; Kieval, "Let Us Never Forget," 123.

Eldridge St.: See Wolfe, *The Synagogues of New York's Lower East Side*, 15–16.

Odessa: George Feifer, "In Search of the Lost Jews of Russia," *The Sunday Times Magazine*, December 13, 1981.

Bayreuth: Harold Rosenthal, "The minyan makers," *Jewish Chronicle*, September 9, 1983.

The Pope: Tullia Zevi, "Pope's historic visit," *Jewish Chronicle*, April 18, 1986.

Western Wall, 2017: www.haaretz.com/israel-news/stop-throwing-us-crumbs-non-orthodox-jewish-leaders-tell-netanyahus-representative-1.5461513

Western Wall, 2018: www.jpost.com/Israel-News/Politics-And-Diplomacy/Women-of-the-Wall-activists-attacked-prayerbook-burned-562463.

#ShowUpForShabbat: Daniel Sugarman, "Khan attends special Shabbat for Pittsburgh," *Jewish Chronicle*, November 9, 2018; Letters to the Editor, *Canadian Jewish News*, November 15, 2018; www.CNN.com/2018/10/29/US/Pittsburgh-synagogue-holocaust-survivor-trend/index.html; Susan Reuben, "Why we need to share our grief," *Jewish Chronicle*, November 2, 2018. On the Tree of Life Synagogue's preparedness for a mass shooting, see Paige Williams, "Under The Gun: In the mass-shooting era, bystanders must act as first responders," *The New Yorker*, April 8, 2019, 31-2.

Tree of Life Synagogue: Anshel Pfeffer, "Rabbis avoid calling Tree of Life a synagogue," *Jewish Chronicle*, November 2, 2018.

21st Century: "Sterile" synagogue: See Rabbi David Wolpe, introduction to Taubman, *Friday Night Live*. "Sterile", boring" synagogue: Rabbi Elyse Goldstein, "We all must build the shul of the future," *Canadian Jewish News*, December 19, 2012.

The Song Shul: Advertisement in *Canadian Jewish News*, August 23, 2018.

Shoresh: Material selected from website: www.shoresh.ca.

Contemporary issues: Daniel Newman, "Filling the Void: New Life for an Alsace Synagogue." *Jewish Renaissance*, July 2018, 12–13.

Challenging assumptions: Jodie Shupac, "Temple Sinai Slichot Service mixes drama and prayer," *Canadian Jewish News*, September 17, 2015.

Let's be honest: Simon Rocker, "A quiet Shabbat morning revolution in the suburbs," *Jewish Chronicle*, 17 March, 2017.

Do shul differently: Ellie Jacobs, "US backs plans 'to do shul differently,'" *Jewish Chronicle*, 28 September, 2018.

Alternative minyanim: Simon Rocker, "Enter the pop-up shuls and made-to-measure minyans," *Jewish Chronicle*, 13 January, 2012.

A crowd-sourcing synagogue: "Shul's name, logo chosen by congregants," *Canadian Jewish News*, October 18, 2012.

Transcending postcodes: "Mishkan: the community beyond borders," *Jewish Chronicle Rosh Hashanah Magazine*, 2017; Simon Rocker, "Moving services," *Jewish Chronicle*, 22 July, 2016; Advertisement, *Jewish Chronicle*, September 2016.

Bibliography

Adler, Elkan Nathan, ed. *Jewish Travellers in the Middle Ages* (1930; reprint, New York: Dover Publications, 1987).

Apple, Raymond. *The Great Synagogue: A History of Sydney's Big Shule*. Sydney: UNSW Press, 2008.

Booth, Charles, ed. *Life and Labour of the People in London*. First series, vol. 3 (1902-4; reprint, New York: AMS, 1970).

Burney, Charles. *The Present State of Music in Germany, The Netherlands, and United Provinces*. Vol. 2. London: T. Becket, 1775.

Ellis, Henry, ed. *Original Letters, Illustrative of English History*. Second series, vol. 4. London: Harding and Lepard, 1827.

Forman, Frieda; Ethel Raicus; Sarah Silverstein Swartz; and Margie Wolfe, eds. *Found Treasures: Stories by Yiddish Women Writers*. Toronto: Second Story Press, 1994.

Frankel, William, and Harvey Miller, eds. *Gown and Tallith: In Commemoration of the Fiftieth Anniversary of the Founding of the Cambridge University Jewish Society*. London: Harvey Miller, 1989.

Glatzer, Nahum N. *Franz Rosenzweig: His Life And Thought*. New York: Schocken, 1961.

Grade, Chaim. *My Mother's Sabbath Days*, trans. Channa Kleinerman Goldstein and Inna Hecker Grade. New York: Shocken, 1987.

Grade, Chaim. *The Yeshiva*, trans. Curt Leviant. 2 vols. Indianapolis: Bobbs-Merrill, 1976-7.

Greenberg, Betty D., and Althea O. Silverman. *The Jewish Home Beautiful*. New York: The National Women's League of the United Synagogue of America, 1958.

Gutter, Pinchas. *Memories in Focus*, The Azrieli Series of Holocaust Survivor Memoirs. Toronto: The Azrieli Foundation, 2018.

Hansen, Waldemar. *The Peacock Throne: The Drama of Mogul India*. New York: Holt, Rinehart and Winston, 1972.

Hanslick, Eduard. *Aus Dem Concertsaal*. Vienna: E.H. Braumüller, 1870.

Howe, Irving, and Eliezer Greenberg. *A Treasury of Yiddish Stories*. London: Andre Deutsch, 1955.

Kalib, Sholom. *The Musical Tradition of the Eastern European Synagogue*. Vol.1. New York: Syracuse University Press, 2002.

Kieval, Robert, "Let Us Never Forget These Favorites," *Proceedings of the 50th Annual Convention* (New York: Cantors Assembly, 1997), 123.

Kobler, Franz, ed. *Letters of Jews Through the Ages*. 2 vols. New York: East and West Library, 1978.

Latham, Robert, and William Matthews, eds. *The Diary of Samuel Pepys*. Vol. 4. Berkeley and Los Angeles: University of California Press, 1971.

Liszt, Franz. *Des Bohémiens et de leur musique en Hongrie*. Leipzig: Breitkopf et Haertel, 1881.

Marcus, Jacob Rader. *American Jewry: Documents. Eighteenth Century*. Cincinnati: The Hebrew Union College Press, 1959.

Metzker, Isaac, ed. *A Bintel Brief: Sixty Years of Letters from the Lower East Side to the Jewish Daily Forward*. New York: Ballantine, 1971.

Meyrink, Gustav. *The Golem*, trans. Mike Mitchell. Sawtry: Daedalus, 2010.

Morgenstern, Sam, ed. *Composers on Music*. New York: Pantheon, 1956.

Nadler, Steven. *Manasseh Ben Israel: Rabbi of Amsterdam*. New Haven: Yale University Press, 2018.

Nathanson, Moshe, ed. *Zamru Lo*. Vol. 3. New York: Cantors Assembly, 1974.

Pessaroff, Sam, "Commissioning Contemporary Composers To Write For The Synagogue: The Historical Contribution of Hazzan David Putterman," *J. Syn. Mus.* 7(4) (1977) 7, 11–12.

Reinach, Théodore, "Sur la Date de la Colonie Juive D'Alexandrie." *Rev. des Etudes Juives* 45 (1902) 161–4.

Roden, Claudia. *The Book of Jewish Food*. London: Viking, 1997.

Rosenbaum, Samuel, "Annual Report of Executive Vice President." *Proceedings of the 48th Annual Convention* (New York: Cantors Assembly, 1995), 37–8.

Rosenblatt, Samuel. *Yossele Rosenblatt: The Story Of His Life As Told By His Son*. New York: Farrar, Straus and Young, 1954.

Rosenfeld, Paul, *Musical Portraits* (1920; reprint, Freeport, N.Y.: Books For Libraries Press, 1968).

Rosse, Jack, "The 'Choral Shool' of Moscow in Pre-Revolutionary Days. As Told by Jack Rosse, Esq." *Cantors' Review* (Association of Ministers Chazanim of Great Britain) 9 (1972) 12-14.

Roth, Cecil. *A History of the Jews in England*. Oxford: Oxford University Press, 1949.

Stein, Erwin, ed. *Arnold Schoenberg: Letters*, trans. Eithne Wilkins and Ernst Kaiser. London: Faber and Faber, 1974.

Taubman, Craig. *Friday Night Live Songbook*. Sherman Oaks, California: Sweet Louise Productions, 1999.

Tissard, François. *De iudaeorum ritibus compendium*. Paris, 1508.

Trollope, Frances. *Vienna and the Austrians*. Vol.1. London: Richard Bentley, 1838.

Vinaver, Chemjo, *Anthology of Jewish Music*. New York: Edward B. Marks Music Corporation, 1955.

Vincent, Isabel. *Bodies and Souls: The Tragic Plight of Three Jewish Women Forced into Prostitution in the Americas.* Toronto: Random House Canada, 2005.

Weiss, Raysh, "A League of Their Own: The Untold Story of the Women's League for Conservative Judaism". *Zeramim: An Online Journal of Applied Jewish Thought.* https://zeramim.org/past-issues/volume-ii-issue-1-fall-20175778/league-untold-story-womens-league-conservative-judaism-raysh-weiss/

Werner, Eric. *A Voice Still Heard.* University Park: Pennsylvania State University Press, 1976.

Wolfe, Gerard R. *The Synagogues of New York's Lower East Side: A Retrospective and Contemporary View.* 2d ed. New York: Fordham University Press, 2013.

Zangwill, Israel, *The King of Schnorrers* (1897; reprint, London: H. Pordes, 1963).

Index

CPSIA information can be obtained
at www.ICGtesting.com
Printed in the USA
LVHW010300210819
628368LV00001B/1

9 781532 667152